DIVING AND SNORKELING GUIDE TO

Cozumel

Cozumel

by George S. Lewbel, Ph.D.,
and the editors of Pisces Books

Pisces Books • New York

Publishers Note: At the time of publication of this book, all the information was determined to be as accurate as possible. However, when you use this guide, new construction may have changed land reference points, weather may have altered reef configurations, and some businesses may no longer be functioning. Your assistance in keeping future editions up-to-date will be greatly appreciated.
  Also, please pay particular attention to the diver rating system in this book. Know your limits!

Library of Congress Cataloging in Publication Data

Lewbel, George S.
  Diving and snorkeling guide to Cozumel.

  Includes bibliographical references.
  1. Scuba diving—Mexico—Cozumel—Guide-books. 2. Skin diving—Mexico—Cozumel—Guide-books. 3. Cozumel (Mexico)—Description and travel—Guide-books. I. Title.
  GV840.S78L49 1984   917.2′64   84-9493
  ISBN 0-86636-033-6

Printed in Hong Kong

10 9 8 7 6 5 4 3 2 1

ACKNOWLEDGMENTS

The authors wish to say "Gracias!" to the following friends for assistance and encouragement in the production of this edition of the guide: Pancho Morales (La Ceiba Hotel, Cozumel); Michele Harrison (Poseidon Venture Tours, Houston); Dick Tompkins (Aqua Safari, Cozumel); Carlos Sierra (Dive Cozumel, Cozumel); Hal Martin (Scuba World, Houston); Karen Young (Underwater Safaris, Houston); Kit Teague; and Sally Sutherland, Kelly Hildreth, and Pancho Contreras.

Staff

Publisher	**Herb Taylor**
Project Director	**Cora Taylor**
Series Editor	**Steve Blount**
Editors	**Carol Denby**
	Linda Weinraub
Assistant Editor	**Teresa Bonoan**
Art Director	**Richard Liu**
Artists	**Charlene Sison**
	Alton Cook

Table of Contents

How to Use This Guide   8

1 Overview of Cozumel   12
Natural History • Cozumel Today • Hotels •
Transportation • Foreign Exchange, Dining, and
Shopping • Documents

2 Diving in Cozumel   22
Some Useful Techniques • Typical Dive Operations • Gorgonian Flats • San
Francisco Reef • La Ceiba Preserve/Trail • Sunken Airplane • International
Pier • Paraiso Reef North • Paraiso Reef South • Chankanab • Beachcomber
Cavern • Yocab Reef • Cardona Reef • Barracuda/San Juan • Columbia
Shallows • Palancar Reef • Santa Rosa Reef • Columbia Reef • Maracaibo
Reef • La Ceiba Dropoff • La Villa Blanca Dropoff

3 Marine Life   80
Spearfishing and Hunting Underwater

4 Safety   84
Diving Accidents • DAN • Common Hazardous Marine Animals

Appendix 1: List of Services   91
Appendix 2: Further Reading   93
Index   94

How to Use This Guide

This guide is designed primarily to acquaint you with a variety of dive sites and to provide information that you can use to help you decide whether a particular location is appropriate for your abilities and intended dive plan (e.g., macrophotography, high-speed drift, etc.). Hardcore divers who travel fully suited-up with fins, masks, snorkels, and BC's in place on the plane (great for over-water flights with nervous traveling companions!) and expect to leap directly from the plane into the water will find this information detailed on a dive-by-dive basis in Chapter 2.

Read the entire chapter (all dives) before diving, since some material common to several sites is not repeated for each one. Chapter 2, "Diving in Cozumel," and Chapter 4, "Safety," should be read first, however, since they cover both routine and emergency procedures and discuss the system used for rating dive sites for beginners, intermediate divers, and advanced divers. Photographers, fishermen, and budding marine biologists will want to refer to the section in Chapter 2 on marine life, which illustrates some of the most common and interesting creatures likely to be seen in Cozumel and summarizes current Mexican fishing regulations that pertain to divers.

Sooner or later, even the most fanatical divers have to come out of the water. Depending on the shore-based facilities, this can be a cause for rejoicing or weeping. As you know, there is an illustrated brochure for virtually every Caribbean diving destination showing the usual beach scenery, palm trees, divers on boats, lobsters on platters, and so on. Perhaps you have been to other locations that offered fine diving but that could have been improved by scraping off everything above the waterline and starting over. This most assuredly is *not* true for Cozumel. Although the diving in Cozumel is spectacular, taking the time to let your gear dry will give you an opportunity to enjoy one of the most charming islands in the Caribbean. Chapter 1, "Overview of Cozumel," offers a brief description of the island's history, geography, scenery, natural history, and some general information on accommodations, services other than diving, shopping, and other useful tips. In the "List of Services," there is a selected list of hotels, dive shops, and dive operators, and will be helpful to divers who need to make their own hotel and diving arrangements upon arrival. It will be most useful to divers planning a first visit.

Lush growth and sheer dropoffs typify the offshore reefs of the island of Cozumel. These formations, such as Palancar and Santa Rosa, are justifiably famous. Since the mid-1950s thousands of divers from all over the world have been drawn to view the massive coral cliffs. Photo: L. Martin. ▶

The Rating System for Divers and Dives

Our suggestions as to the minimum level of expertise required for any given dive should be taken in a conservative sense, keeping in mind the old adage about there being old divers and bold divers but few old bold divers. We consider a *novice* to be someone in decent physical condition, who has recently completed a basic certification diving course, or a certified diver who has not been diving recently or who has no experience in similar waters. We consider an *intermediate* to be a certified diver in excellent physical condition who has been diving actively for at least a year following a basic course, and who has been diving recently in similar waters. We consider an *advanced* diver to be someone who has completed an advanced certification diving course, has been diving recently in similar waters, and is in excellent physical condition. You will have to decide if you are capable of making any particular dive, depending on your level of training, recency of experience, and physical condition, as well as water conditions at the site. Remember that water conditions can change at any time, even during a dive. The rating system we've used is shown schematically in a chart in the chapter, "Diving in Cozumel".

Nestled under the protective arm of Mexico's Yucatan peninsula, Cozumel provides some of the most spectacular diving in the hemisphere.

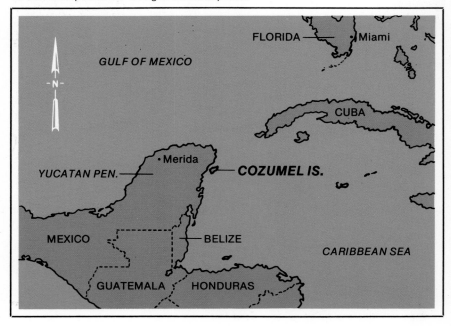

Reef inhabitants, such as this rare and endangered species of pillar coral, are covered in the waterproof guide to the La Ceiba nature trail. The trail's marked observation stations are keyed to entries in the guide.   Photo: G. Lewbel

1

Overview of Cozumel

Cozumel Island is located near the eastern tip of the Yucatan Peninsula in the Mexican State of Quintana Roo. The island is about 30 miles (48 kilometers) long and about 10 miles (16 kilometers) wide. Due to its proximity to the mainland, the center of Mayan culture, the island was under Mayan influence for many centuries. Even today many residents of Cozumel show a striking resemblance to carved and painted images of pre-Columbian Mayans, and many locals still speak a Mayan dialect as well as Spanish. Some Mayan ruins may be found in the jungles on the island, although the most famous and spectacular archaeological sites are on the mainland (e.g., Chichen Itza, Cobah, and Tulum). These sites can be visited on one-day tours leaving from Cozumel; reservations for tours can be made at almost any hotel or at the airport.

The island has long been a favored spot for travelers. In pre-Conquest times it was a religious center for Mayans, and subsequently it was visited by such notables as Hernán Cortez (who conquered Mexico for Spain during the sixteenth century) and a number of pirates who took advantage of the abundant fresh water on the island and the calm, deep waters near the western shore to anchor and rest between raids. More recently, the island has been invaded by thousands of divers seeking clear, warm water. Today Cozumel has a most unusual blend of cultures, successfully integrating divers (nearly all American) with the resort industry of modern Mexico and the local Mayan heritage.

The shallow depths, abundance of light and marine life make Cozumel a treat for divers who are able to visit . Photo: G. Lewbel. ▶

Natural History

Both Cozumel and the peninsula are low-lying terraces of limestone covered with jungle. The limestone is derived largely from coral that has been solidified and compressed into hard rock over the eons. You can see the fossilized imprints of shells and corals from ancient reefs that make up the limestone if you look at it carefully along the shore. Much of the coast of Cozumel (especially along the western side) has no sandy beaches but rather is made up of eroded limestone or "ironshore." On the eastern sides, sandy beaches cover the ironshore in many areas. The limestone is porous, retaining rainwater like a sponge and slowly dissolving. As a result, a halo of fresh water is sometimes seen in the ocean near some spots on the coast. The jungle is dotted with fresh-water springs, caverns, wells, and pools *(cenotes)*, which may contain brackish or fresh water depending on the level of the water table and the amount of seawater that can intrude through passageways in the rock. At the southern tip of the island, salt marshes create a swampy environment that attracts and holds tourists' vehicles like a magnet.

The island is separated from the mainland by a channel only 12 miles (19 kilometers) wide. On most nights, if you look to the west, you can see a few lights of the Yucatan coast from the shores of Cozumel. Most of the mainland coast looks pitch dark at night, however, since most of Yucatan is still solid jungle (yes, the real kind with hanging vines, poisonous snakes, and parrots and monkeys in the treetops); the only clearings are an occasional ranch or farm and the *cenotes*. For that matter, nearly all of Cozumel Island is jungle, too. If you go hiking, look out for snakes and don't sit on fire ant hills. Fire ants are small, ordinary-looking insects that are to other ants as chile peppers are to tomatoes.

Weather. Due to the rather constant temperature of the water currents that sweep around the island, the climate on Cozumel is predictably although not entirely stable. The annual average air temperature is about 80°F (27°C), and you can expect temperatures in the high 80's to low 90's F (bout 32°C) in July and August, and in the mid-70's F (about 24°C) in December and January. Water temperatures range from about 77°–82°F (25°–28°C). However, December and January can see cold fronts from the Continent that can create windy, cloudy, and cold weather. A cooling breeze usually blows day and night. Afternoon thundershowers are common but seldom last more than an hour. Late fall sometimes brings hurricanes to the Caribbean, but their paths usually bypass Cozumel to the east.

Cozumel Island Today

About a third of the western-facing shore of Cozumel has been developed into a dense strip of modern hotels along a single road that runs within a few hundred feet of the beach. The strip is separated by the road from the jungle. Taxis patrol this strip day and night, dueling with brave tourists on mopeds.

The hotel row runs north and south from San Miguel, the only town on the island. San Miguel is a typical small Mexican town in some respects, with tiny shops, narrow streets, and a pretty central plaza. In the last few years, however, San Miguel has had to come to grips with its international position as the main service center for an island besieged with divers year round. By and large, it has made the adjustment gracefully. There are many small, inexpensive hotels in town within walking distance of the plaza, restaurants ranging from very inexpensive to fairly expensive, several department stores and markets, liquor stores, a number of dive shops (look for the red and white divers' flag everywhere), car and moped rental agencies, and the ever-present Mexican curio and handicraft shops.

The larger hotels outside town have their own shops and restaurants, and it's possible to spend your entire vacation without venturing into town if you stay in one of the beachfront resorts. You'll be missing a good bet, though, if you don't go into town at least one evening to shop and look around.

The La Ceiba Hotel, co-owned by Pancho Morales, himself a prominent local diver, is the location of three excellent dive sites and within swimming distance of two others. Photo: S. Blount.

Hotels

Virtually all of the hotels on the island cater to divers. They can be divided fairly easily into two general categories: luxury (resort) hotels and simpler, less expensive hotels. Several condominiums have recently been completed. They tend toward luxury.

The luxury hotels are located along the waterfront to the north and south of town. They generally have every amenity that one would expect in an international facility, including swimming pools, air-conditioned rooms, restaurants, gift shops, and the like. Many of the luxury hotels have dive shops on the premises, and most of them have easy entries and exits (such as concrete steps) at the waterline so that you can go diving right in front of them. Several hotels that have particularly good diving from their own beaches or piers are mentioned in Chapter 2.

The simpler hotels are located in town within several blocks of the plaza. Some are air-conditioned, some have restaurants in them (but are within easy walking distance of dozens of other restaurants), and all are much less expensive than the luxury hotels. The simpler hotels usually do not have dive shops on the premises, but nearly all have some working

Cozumel's International Pier does double duty as a mooring site for cruise ships and an underwater tourist attraction. Built in 1972 and accessible from the La Ceiba Hotel, the pier pilings and construction rubble underneath have become home to a variety of brilliantly colored sponges and fish. Buttery-warm waters and the presence of nocturnal animals such as starfish and octopusses make the pier ideal for night diving. Photo: L. Martin.

arrangement with one or more dive shops so that you can arrange equipment rental and boat diving through them. Most of the simpler hotels are located near the center of town, within walking distance of dive shops.

Transportation

Car Rentals. Rental cars can be arranged by almost every hotel or condominium, but it is not uncommon to have every car on the island reserved. The best procedure is to reserve a rental car through an international company that is represented in the States. Most of the larger companies have an office at the airport; some also have offices at the luxury hotels. Driving is on the right-hand side of the road, Mexican style, with the likely possibility of arrest and detention in case of an accident, so be on the defensive and be sure to buy insurance. If you're feeling brave, the larger hotels and a number of highly visible shops in town (within a block of the plaza) rent mopeds. You'll recognize them by their huge signs and the fleets of motor bikes parked in front. See the section on Documents at the end of this chapter for further information on car rentals.

Taxis. While you can rent a car to get you to shore diving locations or to shops, taxis are abundant and very inexpensive, and you may find it convenient to leave the transportation to them. The cost of a taxi ride is fixed within town and along the hotel strip, and the prices are posted in each cab. If you want to go around to the eastern side of the island, though, renting a car is preferable; you'll want to stop to have a beach all to yourself, and you almost certainly won't be able to summon a cab to pick you up later. There are virtually no phones outside of town and the hotel strip, so before you go adventuring tell someone where you're going, and make sure you can change a flat tire!

Tipping

Tipping in Mexico is similar to tipping in the U.S. The range for excellent service is 10–15%, and the trades relying on tips are those traditional ones that cater to travelers (waiters and waitresses, cab drivers, hotel staff, etc.). Be sure to check your hotel or restaurant bill to see if service is included *(servicio incluido)* in the charges; if it is, no tip is expected.

Foreign Exchange, Dining, and Shopping

Foreign Exchange. Nearly all of the hotels, stores, and restaurants on the island are used to dealing with foreigners. In addition to the divers from the U.S.A., several cruise liners dock at Cozumel every week, disgorging hundreds of tourists. Consequently, U.S. dollars are accepted nearly everywhere at very close to the official exchange rate. Our experience has been that it's not really worth the trouble to try to get a few cents more by standing in line to exchange dollars at the bank unless you're really a high roller. Currency other than U.S. dollars or pesos may present problems, however, and a bank visit may be required. You can buy pesos at many banks and airports in the States as well as in Mexico in case you want to get this out of the way in advance.

The local economy is heavily dependent on divers and other tourists. Street vendors sell fresh fruit, cut to order and served on a stick, in front of the small shops in San Miguel. Excellent buys in handworked silver and ceramics can be had in these shops.
Photo: S. Blount.

Dining. Even if your Spanish is rusty (or nonexistent) you'll have no problem getting what you need on the island. Most restaurants have menus in English and Spanish, and almost every restaurant, store, and hotel has someone on staff or within reach who speaks English. Cozumel may be the easiest place in Mexico to visit if you don't speak Spanish, although any attempts to communicate in Spanish (even high-school Spanish!) will be graciously received and encouraged.

Restaurant dining therefore will present no unusual challenges to visiting divers. Seafood is the island specialty, and fresh conch, lobster, and fish are served proudly by most restaurants. Though temperatures remain warm all year, the dress style all over the island is diver-elegant (i.e., t-shirts or light sports clothes), and you won't need to take your tie or dinner jacket anywhere.

La Turista: Avoiding and Treating It

Perhaps a word of advice on sanitation might be welcome here, given the cost of a diving vacation and the unhappiness of having to sit out a dive due to illness. Throughout most tropical countries (Mexico included), it's a good practice not to consume any water or ice cubes that have not been purified (ask for *agua purificado* or carbonated mineral water, *agua mineral con gaz*). You will also increase your chances of avoiding difficulties if you don't eat salads or uncooked vegetables, peel all fruit, and take a prescription antibiotic just in case.

If worse comes to worst and you catch Montezuma's revenge, there is a pharmacy *(farmacia)* within the large market-department store at the northeast corner of the plaza, and the pharmacy will generally dispense whatever you need, even drugs that are available only on prescription in the States, if you know what to ask for and how to use it. The paranoid diver (ourselves included) has his own doctor set up a medical kit before leaving home, taking into account the possibility of catching the *turista* on the road. Kaopectate® or Pepto-Bismol® works for mild cases, while Lomotil® (prescription required in the U.S.) is your serious "cork-in-a-jar"!

Shopping. With regard to shopping, most consumer goods such as canned or packaged food at markets are imported from the United States. Consequently, don't expect any bargains on American products whatever the peso/dollar exchange rate may be. These goods are purchased with dollars and shipped from the States into Mexico (picking up some taxes along the way). Gourmands note: the shops are used to catering to post-dive munchies fits, and most food stores sell Danish cookies, fancy Dutch and Swiss chocolate bars, and similar vital commodities. Make sure they aren't melted before leaving the store. We once had a heartbreaking experience on a sunny day with a pile of vital, emergency-use-only, raspberry-filled bittersweet candy bars ...

There are many Mexican souvenir items available, and the best buys may be had on these. As in other Mexican locations, high-quality sterling silver jewelry, handmade blankets, hammocks, and serapes, carved onyx chess sets and figurines, and simulated pre-Columbian pottery are sold by most shops. *Caveat emptor* is the rule of thumb, although the stamp "sterling" on silver can almost always be relied on as its use is controlled by the Mexican government. Expect to bargain for souvenir-type items, with the original asking price perhaps double the final selling price, but don't bother haggling in any of the department stores or markets selling imported goods. Lots of souvenirs seem to be designed mainly for divers, such as carvings of sea creatures and turtle-shell combs, rings, and bracelets. Sea turtles are on the Endangered Species List for the U.S., however, and it is highly illegal to import any turtle-shell items into the States. U.S. Customs will seize them (and you, if you try to sneak them in) upon your return.

Documents

A word to the wise about documentation and international travel is included here. To get into Mexico you'll need some proof of citizenship (e.g., passport, birth certificate, voter's registration). If you're bringing along any minors who are not accompanied by *both* parents, you must have a notarized, detailed letter from the absent parent or parents giving you permission to take the child into Mexico for a vacation.

On your arrival in Mexico, you'll be issued a Mexican Tourist Permit— a thin blue-and-pink document complete with signatures and rubber stamps. Don't lose it! You'll need the Permit to leave Mexico, and may be asked to show it at any time by Mexican officials. When you leave Mexico, you'll turn in your Tourist Permit along with a departure tax (save about $5 U.S. for this) if you fly out.

Driver's License. If you plan to rent a car or moped, you'll need your U.S. Driver's License, as well as a major credit card or a giant wad of cash to show you can financially cover any damage to the vehicle.

C-Card. Unless you have your diver's certification card with you, you will not be able to rent tanks or charter boats. In other words, no card, no diving, no fun.

On the northeast tip of the island, near the lighthouse, is a lagoon piled with huge sea turtle shells. Because sea turtles are endangered, it is illegal to import any tortoise shell items into the United States. Photo: S. Blount.

2

Diving in Cozumel

This book describes a number of popular spots and some that are less frequently dived but well worth seeing. Numerous shore dives are listed, and you will find that several fine days can be spent diving from the shore for the cost of a taxi ride or two to entry and exit areas. Some reefs can be dived either from boat or shore, depending on how energetic (or lazy) you feel. Other reefs are best dived by boat.

The branch of the Gulf Stream that sweeps along the north/south-oriented island produces currents that range from barely perceptible to well over three knots. The farther offshore one goes, the stronger the current (usually). The finest diving may be found on the crest of a near-vertical wall that runs the length of the western shore of the island. Since this shore faces the mainland across a narrow channel, the weather there is usually much better for diving than on the eastern shore. On the western side, the lip of the wall is within swimming distance of the shore at some sites, though in others a boat is necessary to reach the wall.

While there are spots on the eastern shore that can be dived during some conditions (e.g., strong west wind), these are not described in this guide because of the difficulty of access and the typically marginal water states.

This book includes comments on typical depths and current conditions and the level of expertise required to dive each site under ideal conditions. You should keep in mind that most of the reefs mentioned are very large, and this dive guide has been compiled to give an overview of what to expect. Consequently, it is possible to find deeper (or shallower) areas than those mentioned as typical of each site, and currents may be much stronger or weaker than anticipated on some days. Shoreline entry and exit spots can change with time, too. Your best source of information about any location will probably be local divers, especially those working for charter dive operators or shops, since they are familiar with the range of possibilities at each site.

Spectacular colors and shapes are to be seen at all depths in Cozumel. Here, blood-red coral, purple sponges, and a delicate brittle star cling to a piling at the International Pier. Photo: L. Martin. ▶

Some Useful Techniques

Since typical conditions on the western side are calm seas but strong currents, drift diving is the norm for both shore and boat diving in most locations, especially those on the wall. As in any open-water situation, you should always carry an emergency signal device such as a whistle, and, if far from shore, an additional device capable of being seen from far away, such as a flare or flashing strobe.

For boat dives, a "live boat" technique is generally used by charter boat captains, who follow divers' bubbles to greet them at the end of the dive. A dive guide is often provided at both ends of a group of divers in order to keep them together while on the reef and to aid pickup at the surface. Be sure to describe your previous experience, swimming abilities, and any special concerns to the divemaster or dive guides on the boat. Given the strong currents around Cozumel, we do not recommend that you rent a boat on your own without a local dive guide and captain. There are special skills required to operate a "live" boat safely around divers, and Cozumel's waters favor using professional operators only.

For shore dives, an exit spot some distance down-current must be selected (and inspected) in advance, since it may be impossible to return to the starting point up-current. Booties and gloves are recommended to deal with ironshore. Many hotel piers can serve as excellent starting and end spots for shore dives. They often feature ideal entrances and exits, such as concrete steps and ladders, and are generally placed in areas sheltered from strong currents. Transportation can be found easily at both the start and end of a dive at hotels. Taxis sometimes park at hotels, waiting for business, and the hotels can always call a taxi for you while you're dripping dry! Don't worry about carrying money with you to cover cabfare at the end of a dive; cabs will wait while you run inside your hotel to get your money.

If you are planning to dive from the shore, be sure not to swim any farther than your capabilities allow for a safe, easy return, and ask the local divers to help you to evaluate water conditions before jumping in. You should also take along a dive flag on a float. The usual current direction is parallel to shore from south to north, with speed increasing as you get farther offshore, but the current sometimes reverses direction and occasionally can take a seaward course. Before your dive, arrange with someone on shore to keep watch along the expected drift pathway and to meet you at your exit point at a given time. That way, if you have any problems en route, help can be summoned promptly.

A small, intricately convoluted coral head rests on the white sand bottom of Paraiso Reef South, one of the most popular sites for snorkelers as well as divers. Photo: G. Lewbel.

The information above should suggest that Cozumel may be enjoyed by divers with a wide range of skill levels. For wall dives in particular, an experienced guide will add considerably to your safety and comfort. The charter dive operators do not, at present, always separate experts from novices on boat dives. For a beginner, to be dropped over a vertical wall in a strong current may be an exciting situation to say the least. Even for the pro there are a few surprises possible. For example, when high-velocity water runs into a coral buttress, zones of rapid upwelling and downwelling develop. Being caught in one of the down-slope currents is similar to being flushed in a gigantic toilet, and divers must be aware of their depths and surroundings at all times.

A little specialized practice on buoyancy control, drift-diving techniques, and deep-diving methods with a qualified instructor can go a very long way toward ensuring a pleasant, safe trip. This instruction should be arranged with the dive shop or charter operator before getting on the boat,

Many hotel piers, such as the one at La Ceiba Hotel, make excellent entrance and exit points for shore dives. Be sure to plan your dive carefully so you know exactly where the exits for your dives will be. Photo: G. Lewbel.

Flat-top dive boats are favored by many dive operators. These allow fairly large groups of divers to suit up comfortably, and are the easiest boats for making entrances and exits. Photo: L.Martin.

however, as dive guides may have their hands full and not be able to offer any instruction without prior appointments. Furthermore, the majority of dive guides on the island are just that—guides—and are not diving instructors. Again, set up any instruction you may need in advance.

We consider diving on or near the lip of sheer walls to be safe only for advanced divers and for intermediate divers, and then only when accompanied by a qualified diving instructor or divemaster. Novices should never place themselves in any situation where loss of buoyancy control can result in rapid depth increases. This translates as advice to keep away from the edges of walls, dropoffs, or buttresses. When high-velocity currents are present, even more caution is indicated. We have rated all *drift* dives (i.e. those for which entry and exit locations differ), except those very near shore (e.g., Paraiso South), as appropriate only for advanced divers and for those intermediates diving with an instructor or divemaster. We have rated some boat dives as appropriate for novices, but only when diving with an instructor or divemaster.

Typical Dive Operations

Dive operators on Cozumel Island vary considerably with respect to their punctuality, the purity of their compressed air, the reliability of their boats, and—most important—their concern for your safety. Some operators employ well-trained guides who are also diving instructors, while others may only hire local divers familiar with reef locations. Some boats carry first-aid kits, some carry oxygen, some have radios, and others don't. Some use tanks that are new, while others use tanks that may not have been hydrostatically tested for fifteen years. Rental gear ranges from "donate-it-to-the-Smithsonian" vintage to near-new, depending on the operator.

At this time, the diving industry on Cozumel is expanding rapidly, and represents a vital economic resource to the island. Your business is anxiously sought by dive operators for this trip and for the next. You do have the right—and, perhaps, the responsibility—to demand first-class service from dive operators in exchange for your money. In the spirit of better, safer diving, we urge you to ask questions about those matters you consider important to you as a diver, and to reward only those operators you are satisfied with by giving your business to them. You can have a positive influence on the future of diving on Cozumel and at the same time increase your safety and enjoyment. For example, we tip a boat dive guide only if he treats our group courteously, provides a complete pre-dive briefing on the site and safety procedures, and keeps a watchful eye on the group in the water. No one likes to think about diving accidents, but consider, just for a moment, how an injury to you or your buddy would be handled, and don't be satisfied with vague answers.

Dive Boat. There are many dive boat operators on the island. Three types of boats are commonly used: 1) open "flat-tops," with broad decks that offer easy suiting up and entries and exits; 2) traditional diesel-powered modified fishing boats (motor sailers) that ride very well in rough weather but tend to be slower than other types of boats; and 3) modern, high-powered runabouts and small cabin cruisers that are fast and stable even in rough seas. You may enjoy the roominess of the flat-tops, or prefer the relaxed pace of the motor sailers, or instead just want to get to and from the dive site as fast as possible. You can make the choice if you ask the operators what kind of boats they run before booking trips. Rather than book all your diving with one operator, you might consider sampling several shops to see how they compare to one another. As we mentioned, there are lots of differences.

Most of the operators offer two-tank trips, providing tanks, backpacks, and weights, with lunch included between dives. The lunch usually is served on San Francisco Beach, a beautiful white sand strip heavily patronized by local Mexican families as well as visiting divers. The most frequently visited part of San Francisco Beach has bathrooms, restaurants

Open-stern fishing boats, like this one, are the common carriers in Cozumel. Local dive shops contract with the captains. Through the local dive shop, you can arrange to be picked up at your hotel's dock, if on the water, or at a convenient beach if you're staying in San Miguel. Photo: S. Blount.

and bars, live music, and good fun. Alternatively, some operators prefer a more remote section of the beach where charcoal-barbecued fish and isolation are the attractions.

Shore Diving. If you are diving from the shore, you will find it extremely easy to rent tanks, backpacks, and weights at the many dive shops in town, at the hotels, and at the well-known Chankanab Lagoon. Most shops rent aluminum cylinders. The older cylinders, at 70 cubic feet and 3000 psi, are presently more common than newer 3000 psi 80's, so look carefully before you rent. Hot, short fills unfortunately are pretty common on Cozumel, although less likely to occur at the larger shops. It's worth the trouble to gauge your rental tank before carrying it away from the shop. If you want to go diving after 5 P.M., plan ahead—most shops close about then.

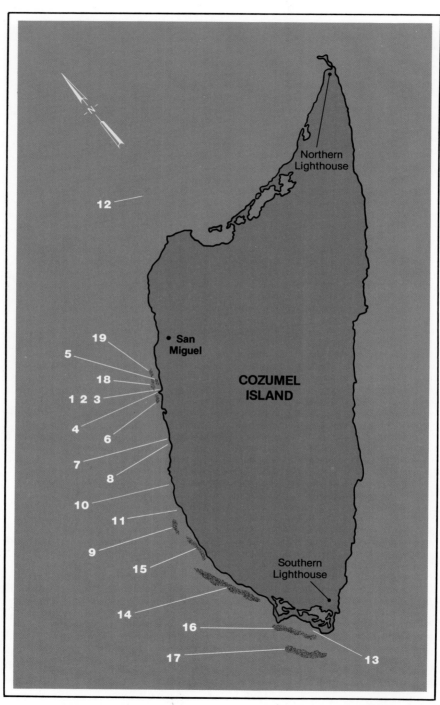

Northern
Lighthouse

12

COZUMEL
ISLAND

• San
Miguel

19
5
18
1 2 3
4
6
7
8
10
11
9
15
14
16
17

Southern
Lighthouse

13

Nestled under the protective arm of Mexico's Yucatan peninsula, Cozumel provides some of the most spectacular diving in the hemisphere.

	Novice Diver	Novice Diver with Instructor or Divemaster	Intermediate Diver	Intermediate Diver with Instructor or Divemaster	Advanced Diver	Advanced Diver with Instructor or Divemaster
1 Gorgonian Flats*	×	×	×	×	×	×
2 La Ceiba Preserve/Trail*	×	×	×	×	×	×
3 Sunken Airplane*	×	×	×	×	×	×
4 International Pier	×	×	×	×	×	×
5 Paraiso North	×	×	×	×	×	×
6 Paraiso South*	×	×	×	×	×	×
7 Chankanab*	×	×	×	×	×	×
8 Beachcomber Cavern	×	×	×	×	×C	×C
9 San Francisco	×	×	×	×	×	×
10 Yocab	×	×	×	×	×	×
11 Cardona			×	×	×	×
12 Barracuda/San Juan					×	×
13 Colombia Shallows*	×	×	×	×	×	×
14 Palancar	×	×	×	×	×	×
15 Santa Rosa			×	×	×	×
16 Colombia			×	×	×	×
17 Maracaibo			×	×	×D	×D
18 La Ceiba Dropff			×	×	×	×
19 La Villa Blanca Dropoff			×	×	×	×

Rating system:
× = Dive is appropriate for a given level of expertise under favorable water conditions. See chapter 2, "Diving in Cozumel," and descriptions of individual dive sites (following in this chapter) for further information.

* = Good snorkeling spot.

C = Specialized training in cavern and cave diving techniques strongly recommended before making this dive.

D = Specialized training in deep diving techniques strongly recommended before making this dive.

When using the accompanying chart see the information on page 10 for an explanation of the diver rating system and site locations.

Gorgonian Flats* 1

Typical depth range	:	10–15 feet (3–5 meters)
Typical current conditions	:	light
Expertise required	:	novice; good snorkeling and skin diving location
Access	:	concrete steps at south base of La Ceiba Hotel pier, or via the small beach cove at the Sol Caribe Hotel

Snorkelers and skin divers will find this an excellent spot to see lots of fish and gorgonians (sea fans), especially the area between the La Ceiba and Sol Caribe Hotels. Scuba divers will probably want to see this area on the way to the La Ceiba Reef Preserve and Trail, or the Sunken Airplane (see text on pp. 36–39). There are full service dive shops renting masks,

Elkhorn and leaf coral and long-spined sea urchins are among the characteristic inhabitants of Gorgonian Flats. Photo: G. Lewbel.

Colorful gorgonian colonies at Gorgonian Flats make excellent backgrounds for photographs of the plentiful fish life there. In the late afternoon, rainbow parrotfish can be found feeding in this area between the Sol Caribe and La Ceiba hotels. Photo: G. Lewbel.

snorkels, and fins at both hotels within a few yards of the water. You can either swim through the channel at the small beach cove at the Sol Caribe Hotel, or walk in and out of the water via the steps at the edge of the La Ceiba Hotel pier.

Near shore, there are large heads of elkhorn coral, under which long-spined sea urchins take shelter (careful!). The beds of sea fans begin at a depth of about 10 feet (3 meters) and continue on seaward, blending into a coral reef at the edge of a sand flat about 30 to 40 feet (9 to 13 meters) deep. There are also big open areas with a few small coral heads; these areas are excellent places to look for large rainbow parrotfishes, especially when the sun is low in late afternoon. You'll see them feeding on the bottom, picking at plants and chunks of coral.

Typical depth range	:	20–60 feet (6–18 meters), but near a wall (depth unlimited)
Typical current conditions:		moderate to strong
Expertise required	:	intermediate (with qualified instructor or divemaster) or advanced
Access	:	boat only

San Francisco Reef is located directly offshore from San Francisco Beach. It consists of a fairly low-profile coral strip on the lip of a dropoff. If you have never made a wall drift dive, San Francisco Reef might be a good one to start with, since the edge of the dropoff is shallower than many of the

A well-camouflaged spider crab is one of the many fascinating inhabitants of San Francisco Reef. Photo: L. Martin.

A bristleworm makes its way across a giant brain coral colony on the lip of San Francisco reef. Compared to other Cozumel reefs, the edge of the wall here is very shallow, coming to within 20 feet (6 meters) of the surface. Photo: G. Lewbel.

other walls on Cozumel. In some places, the lip is as shallow as 20 feet (6 meters), though 50–60 feet (15–18 meters) is more typical. Even if you have lots of experience on walls, you'll really enjoy the extra bottom time you can get on this reef by staying shallow.

The reef is an excellent spot to see filefish, angelfish, trumpet fish, and other common reef species. It is also known for its tentacle-faced *(Stoichactis)* anemones, which look like beds of small green grapes up to a foot across. The many nooks and crannies on San Francisco Reef shelter large lobsters, and you can often find bigeye, sweepers, and other nocturnal fish hiding in the crevices during the daytime. If you stray off the reef and over to the west, you'll be looking down into the dropoff; the white sand to the east is a good place for stingrays and conch.

Typical depth range	:	20–40 feet (6–12 meters)
Typical current conditions	:	light
Expertise required	:	novice; the site is often used for training beginners and for checkout dives
Access	:	concrete steps at south base of La Ceiba Hotel Pier

This shallow coral reef is mostly within a few hundred feet of shore, making it an ideal first dive or warmup dive. A paved driveway on the northern edge of the hotel grounds provides easy access to the pier. There is a full-service dive shop at the end of the driveway, and a shaded pavilion next to the jumping-off spot where you can suit up out of the sun. There is also a freshwater tank for washing your gear inside the pavilion, and a shower for washing yourself off next to the hotel swimming pool.

A patch of red encrusting sponge is growing over this mountainous star coral along the La Ceiba underwater nature trail. A waterproof trail guide is available at the LaCeiba dive shop.
Photo: G. Lewbel.

Night Diving Off the Pier

This area is near-perfect for night dives as a result of pier lighting, easy entries and exits, relatively shallow and flat bottom, and typically calm conditions. The hut at the base of the pier usually is lit at night, making it an ideal spot for suiting up after dark. If you advise the hotel front desk that you are making a night dive, they can generally make sure that the lights on the end of the pier stay on to guide you back. Photographers looking for basket stars spread out and feeding in the dark will find large numbers of them perched on top of gorgonians, especially at depths from 15–25 feet (5–8 meters), about halfway between the La Ceiba pier and the next one to the north, the Sol Caribe Hotel Pier.

The closest reef in front of the hotel runs roughly parallel to shore along a ridge at about 25–30 feet (8–10 meters) that separates a sand flat (about 40 feet or 12 meters) from a gorgonian bed. Next to shore you'll see elkhorn coral (especially south of the pier), then a gorgonian bed, then large stands of lettuce or plate corals, and finally a row of outcrops of star corals and other common species mixed with various small sponges. The fish that school around the pier are used to receiving handouts, and you'll probably be mobbed by bermuda chub if you take along some pieces of bread. The shallow coral heads in 10 feet (3 meters) of water are patrolled by territorial damselfish, so don't be surprised by a nip from an outraged homeowner if you linger nearby.

If you're interested in reef animals and plants, the La Ceiba dive shop can sell or lend you a copy of a Waterproof Trail Guide and Map to take along on your dive. The Guide, keyed to 15 permanently marked underwater stations, is designed to teach you about coral reef ecology and how to recognize common reef animals and plants. The Trail was installed several years ago, and many of the stations need re-labeling and new buoys; at last viewing it was in mediocre shape. It's worth snorkeling over the Trail to see if the buoys are there before buying the Guide. If you want help along the way, the dive shop personnel can point out the Trail to you. The Trail starts at the Sunken Airplane and includes sections of large coral heads, sponges, pillar coral, very large gorgonians, and sand-flat animals such as the nest-building sand tilefish.

Typical depth range	:	30–40 feet (10–12 meters)
Typical current conditions	:	light
Expertise required	:	novice; the site is often used for training beginners and for checkout dives
Access	:	concrete steps at south base of La Ceiba Hotel pier, or via the small beach cove at the Sol Caribe Hotel

The Sunken Airplane lies on sandy bottom about 40 feet (12 meters) deep, at the seaward edge of a low-profile coral ridge less than two hundred yards (175 meters) from shore. It is almost directly off the La Ceiba dive shop and is marked with a small surface buoy. The airplane (an old twin-engine prop plane) was placed on the bottom for a Mexican disaster movie. It has since been overturned by storms but is mostly intact. It is an outstanding spot for photography. Many fish have made it their home. Its surface remains fairly clean due to the scraping bites of parrotfish, whose toothmarks can be seen on the metal along with the graffiti of thoughtless divers. Also, look for purple patches of sergeant-major eggs on the plane. They'll be guarded by aggressive sergeant-majors.

There are full service dive shops at both La Ceiba and Sol Caribe

Hedgerows of gorgonians scattered among clumps of coral on a sandy bottom (left) lead from the pier at the La Ceiba Hotel out to the sunken airplane. The underwater nature trail here is also an exciting spot for a night dive, when parrot fish can often be seen sleeping inside their translucent cocoons.
Photo: G. Lewbel.

Placed here as a prop for a movie by film director Ramon Bravo, this sunken twin-engine airplane was saved for divers by the owner of the La Ceiba Hotel. Storms overturned the plane so that its extended landing gear now point to the surface, but it still makes a dramatic backdrop for photographs. Photo: G. Lewbel.

Hotels, and the shop personnel can point out the buoy to you if you can't spot it. Enter and exit either at the La Ceiba pier or by swimming out the small cove at the Sol Caribe Hotel. If there is any current running, you might consider jumping in at the up-current site, swimming out to the airplane, and exiting at the down-current site to save yourself some swimming. The airplane marks the starts of the Underwater Trail described in the preceding section. The gorgonian flats between shore and the airplane are excellent for snorkelers and skin divers.

The Sunken Airplane (a Snorkelers View)

If you're snorkeling or skin diving on the Gorgonian Flats and the current isn't too strong—and if you're in good shape— you may want to swim out to the underwater trail, or to the Sunken Airplane. From the surface you can see a large number of scuba divers there, and unless the water is very dirty you will be able to see the entire plane from the surface. It's a bit deep for most skin divers to reach (about 35 feet or 10 meters to the upper parts of the plane), and you should be very careful not to get snagged in one of the several ropes and lines attached to the plane.

Typical depth range	:	15–70 feet (5–20 meters)
Typical current conditions	:	light to moderate, occasionally strong, increasing with distance from shore
Expertise required	:	novice (with qualified instructor or divemaster) or intermediate
Access	:	concrete steps at south base of La Ceiba Hotel Pier

The International Pier was installed in 1978 on a sand bottom. It has a large accumulation of construction material and rubble beneath it, and many interesting marine organisms have grown up on it. You'll find vase

A yellow stingray cruises the sand flats near the International Pier. Moray eels and sea biscuits are also often seen in the area.   Photo: L. Martin.

A brittle starfish clings to a patch of red sponge encrusting a piling under the International Pier. The tan-green patches surrounding the sponge are fire coral, which isn't a true coral at all, but a relative of the jellyfish. It's a good idea to wear a wetsuit and gloves when diving around the pier as contact with the fire coral could result in a painful sting.
Photo: G. Lewbel.

sponges, blood-red encrusting sheet sponges up to six feet (2 meters) across, anemones, and so forth. The prevailing current direction is from south to north, and the attached animals on the pylons have grown in a crooked fashion, leaning into the current like trees in the wind. Fire coral forms thin, wide layers on the concrete, so don't touch anything that looks like tan paint! Schools of fish take shelter in the huge canyons between vertical pylons, and many small barracudas hover around the outside of the International Pier. Photographers will find this site quite eerie for shooting, a combination coral reef and concrete jungle.

As striking as the International Pier is at daytime, it is even more spectacular at night. On a single dive you may find sleeping pufferfish and barracudas, open orange-ball anemones, huge sea cucumbers, prowling moray eels, and large brown sea-biscuits (sand-dollar relatives) on the surrounding sand flats, and other nocturnal fishes milling around. Furthermore, you'll probably use up all your film in the first five minutes of the dive when you see the intense red colors of the sponges on the concrete pylons.

The best access to the International Pier is via the steps at the La Ceiba Hotel pier, when the current is running south-to-north. Stay near the shore on the way to the International Pier to keep out of the main stream, and then ride the current back to the La Ceiba pier after the dive. The base of the International Pier is in about 15 feet (5 meters) of water, and the seaward end is in about 60–70 feet (18–22 meters). Depths increase gradually offshore until a few hundred feet past the end of the pier, where you come to the lip of a drop-off. As you get farther offshore, the current strength usually increases, and it may be necessary to "leapfrog" from one pylon to the next to stay by the International Pier. The pylons are very large, though, and it shouldn't be too difficult to stay in relatively calm water on the down-current sides of the pylons.

Due to the lack of convenient exits immediately south of the International Pier, we recommend that you dive there only when currents are absent or running gently from south to north. You can also dive at the end of a beach dive at Paraiso Reef South when currents are running from the south, if your bottom time and air permit. In an emergency you could exit at the rocks on the northern edge of the base of the International Pier, but be prepared for problems with the authorities as you're not legally permitted to use this location.

Hazards

Various ships including ferries, work boats, and cruise liners dock at the International Pier. While they do provide some lost items for divers to find (long-stemmed wine glasses sometimes litter the bottom), these vessels may present an extreme hazard to divers on or near the surface. Stay well clear of any boat traffic and stay near the bottom when approaching or leaving the area. Do not surface around the International Pier; keep in mind that vessels may arrive while you are under water. Do not make this dive if any vessels are docked at the International Pier or moving in the vicinity. Before making a dive near the International Pier, you should check with the Mexican authorities in the office at the base of the International Pier to advise them of your intentions, and to see if diving is permitted; sometimes it is, sometimes it isn't.

The pilings and concrete rubble under the International Pier have become an oasis of riotous color amid the drab surrounding sand flats. Tube sponges, encrusting sponges, orange ball anemones and other attaching organisms coat this underwater scrap heap. Photo: G. Lewbel.

Typical depth range	:	40–50 feet (12–15 meters)
Typical current conditions	:	light to moderate, occasionally strong
Expertise required	:	intermediate
Access	:	concrete steps at south base of La Ceiba Hotel pier, or via the small beach cove at the Sol Caribe Hotel

Paraiso (Paradise) Reef is a long series of backbone-like strips of coral running parallel to the shore. The series can be intersected by swimming perpendicular to the shore out to a depth of about 40–50 feet (12–14 meters). If you exceed this depth you've missed the reef and gone too far, and you should turn around and head back toward shore. Paraiso Reef North lies just seaward of the sand flat that is marked at its shoreward edge by the Sunken Airplane (see the description of Gorgonian Flats). To find Paraiso North, swim from the plane straight offshore toward the wall. You can usually see the reef from the surface as the first dark streak

The Mexican federal government made the eastern shore of Cozumel a national marine park to help protect the many unusual species found here, such as the Cozumel splendid toadfish. No spearfishing or taking of live animals is permitted in the park. Photo: G. Lewbel.

Waters from the Gulf of Mexico rush through the narrow, 12-mile (19 kilometer) channel that separates Cozumel from the Yucatan Peninsula. This flow creates the currents that sweep the western shore. The constant flushing improves visibility and helps animals such as corals and this basket sponge, which feed by filtering micro-organisms from the water, to grow to stupendous size. Photo: G. Lewbel.

encountered after leaving the plane. It is about a five minute swim from the plane.

The reef itself consists of large coral heads, and sponges up to 6 feet (2 meters) in diameter. Large schools of iridescent blue chromis fishes form clouds above the reef, and if you hunt carefully around the sandy bases of the big coral heads you may catch a glimpse of the blue-, white-, and yellow-striped splendid toadfish. Paraiso North is not large—a few hundred feet long—and is probably best visited as part of a longer dive, perhaps starting at this reef and proceeding inward to end near the airplane.

Paraiso North is far enough offshore to be subject to the influence of strong currents, and if you're headed to or from this reef you may have to correct for drift. If you're carried northward by the current you will find the handiest exit at the Sol Caribe pier. If you're carried southward, you can work your way inward along the large concrete International Pier (see the International Pier Section for cautions) and exit at the La Ceiba pier. There is often boat traffic between Paraiso North, the Sol Caribe, and the La Ceiba, so if you're on or near the surface you should keep alert and be prepared to get out of the way of vessels that may not see or avoid you.

Paraiso Reef South* 6

Typical depth range	:	35–45 feet (11–14 meters)
Typical current conditions	:	moderate
Expertise required	:	novice (with qualified instructor or divemaster) or intermediate
Access	:	from the second telephone pole (#56) on the shore just north of the yacht basin *(caleta)* on the north side of the El Presidente Hotel, or via boat

Paraiso (Paradise) Reef South consists of two long ridges of coral running parallel to shore end-to-end, at depths of about 35–40 feet (11–12 meters), surrounded by sand. It is frequently visited by charter boats as a second dive after a deeper wall dive. It is also a favorite among dive operators for night dives, since it is a short boat ride from most hotels, and is fairly shallow. It may also be reached easily from the shore. It's a bit deep for most skin divers, but the nearshore ridge is a good reef to snorkel over and watch scuba divers. Look out for boat traffic!

Crevices at the base of coral heads on Paraiso Reef South serve as the toehold for giant sea cucumbers which, during the night, stretch out to two meters (six feet) in length. When the current is running, Paraiso South is a good place to get some experience in drift dive techniques before tackling the deeper walls offshore. Photo: G. Lewbel.

Red and orange sponges splash the sides of a coral head with their brilliant color. Reef predators lurk in the crevices waiting for unwary prey to pass by. Photo: L. Martin.

Paraiso Reef South is home to many tame fish that have been fed by dive guides. If you're hoping to see large, bizarre filefish, or French and gray angels within arms' reach, you'll probably not be disappointed. The coral formations are medium-sized and this entire reef is relatively low in profile. The small crevices at the bases of the coral heads shelter many squirrelfish during the daytime, and serve as "toeholds" for the six-foot-long (2 meters) sea cucumbers that stretch out on the sand at night to feed. The reef is ideal for photographers, since depth control on the fairly level bottom is far simpler than on any of the walls. If you're planning to make a wall dive during your stay on Cozumel, you'll find that when the current is running Paraiso South is a good place to get some experience in drift diving techniques over level bottom before you hit the dropoffs.

We recommend this dive only when there is no current, or when the current is running from south to north, since most of the reef stretches to the north of pole #56. The easiest access to this dive is to leave your car (if you have one) at La Ceiba Hotel, and take a taxi around the *caleta* just north of the El Presidente Hotel. The road will pass the harbor and then return to the coast. Get out at the second telephone pole (#56), walk into the water (sand and a few rocks), and swim straight offshore over sand

and seagrass until you intersect the reef (about 5–10 minutes' swim). The first major dark streak out from shore is seagrass; the second is the reef.

If there is no current, you can dive the southern part of the reef and exit at the entry spot. If, by chance, you get caught in a current running to the south over Paraiso Reef South, you can exit at the yacht basin or at the El Presidente, but be extremely careful of boat traffic! If the current is running to the north, drift along the coral ridge with it. The first ridge is several hundred yards long, and ends abruptly at its northernmost point in sand. If your air and bottom time permit, continue swimming toward the north, but angle to your left (westward or seaward) about 30° when you leave the first ridge. You will come to the southern tip of the second ridge within a minute or two. The second section parallels the shore, but slightly seaward of the first, and is about the same in length. The second section also ends in sand at its northern tip.

If you surface at this point, you will not be near any convenient exit spot, but you will be drifting toward an excellent one—the La Ceiba pier. Continue to the north, pass through the International Pier at its shoreward end (see **Hazards** in the section on the International Pier), and walk out at the steps on the southern edge of the La Ceiba pier. If you have enough air and bottom time left to stay down for some or all of this distance, you can be sure of coming out at the right spot if you simply watch your depth and stay over bottom that is about 25 feet (8 meters) deep. This depth contour will pass through the International Pier about a quarter of its length out from shore. En route from Paraiso Reef South to the International Pier, you will pass over some interesting seagrass beds harboring giant conch shells, turkey-wing oysters, and pen shells.

A school of French-striped grunts swarms through a crack between coral boulders on Paraiso (Paradise) Reef South. Many of the fish on Paraiso are quite tame, as they are fed often by local divemasters. Photo: L. Martin.

Typical depth range	:	10 feet (lagoon)–35 feet (nearshore coral heads (3–11 meters)
Typical current conditions	:	none (lagoon); light (nearshore coral heads)
Expertise required	:	novice; good snorkeling and skin diving location
Access	:	walk into the water down concrete steps at the edge of a parking lot

Chankanab is one of the most popular shore dives on the island, having a shallow, saucer-like lagoon on the inshore side of the road. The lagoon is connected to the sea by a short tunnel through which divers can easily swim. The lagoon is ideal for training purposes, having a soft, smooth bottom. It is fairly featureless, and experienced divers use it only as an entry and exit spot by swimming to the ocean via the tunnel.

Chankanab boasts facilities for gear rental and air fills, and is a popular weekend location for island residents due to new picnic facilities and shops selling snacks. It's also one of the more common sites for moped crashes due to the large, economy-sized speed bumps installed in the road, so be careful!

Lime green tunicates are taking over this coral head at Chankanab Lagoon. Because it is protected, the Lagoon is ideal for night diving, when octopusses, eels and other nocturnal creatures emerge from their crevices and wander over the sandy bottom. Photo: G. Lewbel.

A juvenile spotted drum hovers over a solitary coral colony at Chankanab Lagoon. The still waters of the Lagoon make it a prime spot for viewing small tropicals. Photo: G. Lewbel.

On the seaward side of the highway, concrete steps and ladders provide extremely easy access to the ocean. The bottom immediately adjacent is about 10 feet (3 meters) deep. There are large schools of tame fish—especially grunts and snappers—that can nearly always be found under large ledges within a few yards of the steps. Photographers will find these fish cooperative and very used to divers, since they've appeared on several posters.

If you swim south along the shore in about 15 feet (5 meters) of water, you'll come to a sculptured bronze madonna placed on a coral head by local dive guides. The area just offshore has tall patch reefs separated by sand channels. The bases of the coral heads are especially good spots to find spotted drums and jacknife fishes. Local tourist interests have placed a small wrecked fishing boat on the bottom just a few hundred feet off the steps (look for the mast sticking out of the water), and an assortment of old cannons and anchors on the sand flats near shore. All in all, this dive must be considered one of the best on the island for beginners in terms of easy access, diversity of marine life, and convenient facilities.

Beachcomber Cavern 8

Typical depth range	:	10 feet –35 feet (3–11 meters)
Typical current conditions	:	access and cavern entrance, light to none; inner portion, unknown
Expertise required	:	access, novice; outer cavern, advanced with specialized training in cavern or cave diving; inner portion (cave), not recommended
Access	:	steps at Chankanab, or by boat

A mass of silver fingerlings boils out of the entrance to Beachcomber Cavern. While inside, the small nooks and crannies protect them from larger predators.   Photo: L. Martin.

Just to the south of the main entrances/exits at Chankanab are several entrances to a large cavern that lead to a cave which penetrates the island for an unknown distance. The site is often called Beachcomber Cavern in memory of a fine seafood restaurant (the Beachcomber) which used to sit above the entrances. The restaurant has since been removed, but the site can be found easily without this landmark.

To get to the entrances, swim on the surface a few hundred feet south (parallel to shore) from Chankanab, staying close to shore until you are facing a large channel-like cut in the shore. Face the shore and you will see a narrow boat channel about 20 feet (6 meters) wide and about 10-15 feet (3-5 meters) deep. It's open on the seaward side and comes to an abrupt end about 50 feet (15 meters) in from the shoreline. You'll be looking at the mouth of it from the seaward side. There has been some move to reconstruct a building next to the channel, so by the time you read this there may be a structure on the left of the boat channel. The main entrance (and exit) to the cavern is just to the left of the cut, on the north side of the rocks that mark the northern edge of the cut. The main entrance is shaped like an inverted triangle, about 10-15 feet (3-5 meters) on a side. There are several alternative entrances and exits on the north side of the boat channel. Most of these openings are large enough for several divers to pass through side-by-side, but if there are any waves or swells you should stay out of the channel to avoid getting beaten around by sloshing water.

Hazards

Divers are cautioned that specialized training and equipment for cavern or cave diving techniques are essential to enter the cavern or cave safely. If you do not have this training and equipment, stay outside the entrances. If you bring a flashlight to the entrances, you will be able to see nearly all of the outer cavern without having to go inside yourself.

The cave has not yet been mapped, although a few local divers have penetrated it for some distance. Due to lack of information about the inner portion, the authors must recommend strongly against entering any sections of the cave except for the outer cavern, that is, the area in which divers can remain within sight of and immediate reach (one breath) of an exit to the outside. Diving the inner portion should be only by experts equipped and trained for exploratory cave diving.

The main entrance to the outer cavern is usually filled with small, silvery fish that form a solid-looking curtain from surface to bottom and from side to side. The curtain will part dramatically as you swim through. Both the main and alternative entrances open into the outer cavern. The outer cavern consists of a large central room about 20–30 feet (6–10 meters) in diameter and about 10 feet (3 meters) high, supported by numerous pillars. The outer cavern ceiling does not enclose any airspaces, but has some small holes (too small for a diver to fit through) that allow beams of sunlight to get through in spots. Several dark, smaller side rooms open onto this central room, and tunnels lead to the inner portion of the cave. The outer cavern and the inner cave have areas of soft, silty bottom that can be resuspended in the water by swimming, so be very careful not to stir up the bottom or you'll lose your visibility! Within the dark cavern you'll be able to see a variety of nocturnal fish (glassy sweepers, bigeyes, glasseye snappers) and possibly a large grouper or two taking a nap during the day. A few urchins simetimes hide near the entrances in the shadows, so use your lights before touching down.

Fungus gives this brain coral its variegated effect. Photo: G. Lewbel.

Glassy sweepers hover just inside the mouth of Beachcomber Cavern. With their oversized eyes, these hatchet-shaped fish prefer the semi-darkness of the cave to the dazzling brilliance of the daytime reef.   Photo: L. Martin.

The Green Mirror

This cavern is famous for a peculiar hydrologic phenomenon that can result in some amazing photographs. Fresh water has saturated the island and, in some locations such as this, seeps back into the sea as if from a sponge. The fresh water is usually colder than the ocean, but it is so much less dense than salt water that it floats on top if protected from turbulence. The cavern provides this protection, allowing a *reverse thermocline* with warmer water below colder water. The fresh water usually forms a brilliant green-colored band a few feet thick on the surface. Sometimes it even produces a mirror-like reflective layer three or four feet (one meter) beneath the surface. Try to see it on your way in before your bubbles and turbulence have disturbed the layer. It's most visible from within the cavern, looking outward through the entrances. After you leave the outer cavern exits you can feel the cold, fresh water on the surface, and see the shimmering mixing layer where the salt and fresh water combine.

Typical depth range	:	50–70 feet (15–20 meters)
Expertise required	:	intermediate (with qualified instructor or divemaster) or advanced
Typical current conditions:		moderate to strong
Access	:	boat

Yocab (also spelled Yucab on some maps) is sometimes dived as a second dive of the day on boats, as it is possible to see a good deal of the reef without exceeding 50 feet (15 meters). Yocab is strongly recommended to those who like the reef running parallel to the current direction (north/south) and surrounded by brilliant white sand bearing large ripple marks that can be attributed to the strong current that usually sweeps over the area from south to north. Large coral heads stick out of the sand to a height of 5–10 feet (2–3 meters); on the down-current sides of these heads divers will find some refuge from the current and a truly marvelous collection of animals also hiding out in the backwaters. The down-current northern ends of coral heads have been sculptured and weathered by sand scour, and many caves and ledges there harbor schools of fish, large

Smooth trunkfishes and an abundance of other reef creatures can be found hiding from the prevailing current in the undercuts on Yocab Reef. The current generally runs from south to north, and the northern sides of the large coral mounds are marked by scoured-out tunnels, arches and caves. Photo: L. Martin.

Coral heads at Yocab Reef extend up five to ten feet (two to three meters) above the sand bottom at 50 feet (17 meters). Many of the heads exhibit a dazzling array of colorful growth, with several varieties of sponges, corals and gorgonians sharing a single boulder. Photo: L. Martin.

lobsters, crabs, and the like. Photographers probably will be frustrated by the current in most spots, but may shoot down "on the deck" in the eaves of the coral heads. Fish will be seen drifting along with divers on days when the current is strong! Very large white-spotted and scrawled filefish frequent Yocab Reef.

Yocab Reef comes to a distinct northern end, marked by a huge coral mound at about 60 feet (18 meters). Beyond this mound the sand slopes rapidly downward toward the wall, and divers will want to make their ascents on sighting this mound at the tip of the reef. As with other drift dives, it is important to stay together with your guides or divemasters, since charter boats usually drift above groups, following their bubbles and picking up all divers together at the end of the dive.

Typical depth range	:	20–45 feet (6–14 meters)
Typical current conditions:		light
Expertise required	:	novice (with qualified instructor or divemaster) or intermediate
Access	:	boat only

Cardona Reef is located a short distance north of San Francisco Reef, too far offshore for a beach dive. It is a good choice for a second boat dive, since most boat operators stop for lunch at nearby San Francisco Beach after visiting Palancar, Santa Rosa, or Colombia. It's a very worthwhile spot, too, if you've already had enough parrotfishes and giant coral heads for the time being. Cardona might be considered a connoisseur's reef, mainly interesting to divers looking for unusual species of fish. Bring a flashlight on this dive. Cardona is a low-profile reef that has relatively few big coral heads, but instead is better known for its long ledges and overhangs. Most of these ledges parallel the shoreline, forming a series of ridges.

If you're used to diving in cold water where there are a lot of algae and you've been wondering where the plants are on coral reefs, look under these ledges. You'll find bright green, wingnut-shaped algae hanging down in areas of reduced light.

Barred cardinalfish hide among the miniature spires of a colony of finger coral at Cardona Reef. The striped spines of a long-spine urchin, another hiding place favored by the elusive cardinalfishes, can be seen at lower right. Photo: G. Lewbel.

The underside of many of the ledges at Cardona Reef are covered with green algae. Nocturnal fish, such as squirrelfish and glassy sweepers often hide in the dark recesses beneath these ledges during the day. Photo: G. Lewbel.

Nocturnal Fishes by Day

The ledges at Cardona Reef provide shelter for some very large schools of nocturnal fish that hide under the overhangs. As a general rule, you can recognize nocturnal fish by two characteristics: first, they're hiding in caves and other dark places during the daytime; and second, they have big eyes with large pupils for effective night vision. Look for the hatchet-shaped glassy sweepers, the red-and-silver-barred glasseye snappers, and a variety of squirrelfishes. Cardinalfishes are also easy to find at Cardona, though they often hide among the spines of sea urchins. If you're taking pictures, you'll probably be able to get close enough to these small, beautiful fishes for a good strobe-lit shot, since many of the ledges are very large and roomy enough to lie beneath.

Typical depth range	:	60–80 feet (18–25 meters)
Expertise required	:	advanced
Typical current conditions:		strong
Access	:	boat only

Barracuda Reef is a high-current area of fairly flat bottom but with a wide variety of scenery. It is an ideal spot for a drift dive, as there is relatively little vertical relief, so buddies can stay together easily and everyone can move downstream at roughly equal speed. At its southern end it consists of patch reefs surrounded by sand. The ripple marks in the sand are some-

times 6 feet (2 meters) high, attesting to the 2–3 knot currents that are not uncommon here. On a calm day when the current is not running this area seems to collect very large barracudas that hang motionless in the water, being cleaned by other fish. More typical conditions, however, will rapidly transport divers over a great deal of terrain in a hurry. The northern portion of the area is sometimes called San Juan Reef. Most of San Juan Reef consists of a huge bed of finger coral and flat brown sheet sponges that seems to stretch for miles at about 60–70 feet (18–20 meters). Toward the northern end of the reef, a large mound of coral ("Kit's Mound") several hundred feet across and about 30 feet (10 meters) high rises from the plain, and a natural amphitheater, "Pino's Bowl," on the northern side of it provides refuge from the current. In this bowl, huge schools of horse-eye jacks are sometime present, and nurse sharks hide under ledges at the base of the bowl. Bottom depth increases rapidly to the north of this bowl and on either side of San Juan Reef.

San Juan Reef is seldom visited by charter operators due to the current and to its location at the northern end of the island far from most of the other more common sites. It is worth asking for on a day when the current is strong and there are only advanced divers in your group. As at other high-current locations, it is not possible to swim up-current to rejoin buddies or other divers, so do stick closely together with partners and guides or divemasters so that you can be picked up as a group at the end of the dive by the drifting boat. The reef is not near any convenient shoreline, and not far from the tip of the island, so if you get separated from your group your next stop may be Texas! In particular, watch your depth, since on either side of San Juan Reef and to the north the bed of coral slopes into deeper water, and due to its relatively low relief the change may not be obvious unless you are keeping an eye on your gauge while moving rapidly along the bottom. Current strength in the area of Kit's Mound may exceed four knots (about 2 meters/second).

◀

Because it's a long distance from the more common dive areas along the southern shore, Barracuda Reef/San Juan Reef is not often dived by the charter boat operators. The current is typically very strong here, up to four knots at times. On days when the current is not running, large schools of barracudas may be found hanging motionless in the water as they are cleaned by smaller fish.

Colombia Shallows

Typical depth range	:	20–40 feet (6–12 meters)
Typical current conditions:		light
Expertise required	:	novice (with qualified instructor or divemaster) or intermediate
Access	:	boat only

Colombia Shallows is one of the most spectacular (and seldom-dived) areas on the island. Colombia Shallows is inshore of Colombia Reef. An outstanding two-tank day of diving would start on the wall at Colombia

At Colombia Shallows, star coral colonies the size of a two-story house rise from the bottom to within a few feet (one meter) of the surface. The tortuous, winding passages between these buttresses are lined with star corals which have grown into large, flat plates in order to catch the scarce sunlight in these dark canyons. Photo: G. Lewbel.

Fabulous Shallow Buttresses

Colombia Shallows is made up of huge vertical buttress formations of star coral that rise from a sand bottom at about 40 feet (12 meters) to within a few feet (one meter) of the surface. The buttress are surrounded by extensive seagrass meadows inhabited by large, tame sand tilefish. There are many channels between the buttresses, and diving this reef is similar to flying between two-story houses. The walls of Colombia Shallows are so steep that they create dark canyons between them, and if you look carefully in shadowy places you'll see star corals that have grown into big, flat plates. The plates act as solar collectors, designed to catch what little light comes their way. The tops of many of the coral buttresses have beautiful small thickets of staghorn and elkhorn coral on top of them. Queen angelfish and spotted drums are common here, too.

and move in to the Shallows for a second dive. However, Colombia Shallows is rarely visited because most boat operators prefer to take divers to Paraiso, Yocab, or other more northerly reefs (near lunch and home port) on their second dive of the day. Many of the charter boats don't carry two tanks per diver, and stop at San Francisco Beach between dives to change tanks and have lunch. These boats almost certainly will not turn around and run south to Colombia Shallows after lunch, so if you want to dive these southerly reefs back-to-back, be sure to make the necessary arrangements before leaving the dock.

Colombia Shallows is a good area for beginners, since currents tend to be light and there's lots of clear space to sit down on sand and between walls of coral. It's a great place to practice hovering. It's like a miniature Palancar Reef without hordes of other divers. Furthermore, the restricted bottom depth lets photographers take wall-type shots without fear of dropping off into an abyss while focusing! Since the area is not often dived, coral and sponges are virtually untouched and intact. Snorkeling is excellent above the coral heads, but look out for boat traffic!

Typical depth range	:	40 feet (12 meters) minimum to unlimited (wall)
Expertise required	:	intermediate (with qualified instructor or divemaster) or advanced
Typical current conditions:		moderate to strong
Access	:	boat only

Palancar Reef, the most famous on the island, is renowned for its towering coral buttresses. Similar in topography to Colombia Reef, Palancar is a long stretch of apartment-house-sized columns reaching as shallow as 30–40 feet (10–12 meters) in some areas but anchored on the edge of a vertical dropoff. Between the columns are white sand channels and caves on the sheer sides of the buttresses. It is possible to stay shallow at Palancar by not descending between buttresses or along the seaward faces, but most of the diving is along the outer wall.

An especially popular area of Palancar, called the Horseshoe *(la Herradura)*, has been the subject of many photographic studies and posters. Another excellent area for a second dive is Palancar Gardens, which has miniature buttresses, canyons, and terraces, with dropoffs starting as shallow as 30 feet (10 meters). It is not possible to "see Palancar" in

Perhaps the most famous of all Cozumel reefs is Palancar. Towering columns of coral line the edge of a sheer wall that drops from 40 feet (12 meters) at the tops of the columns into more than a hundred fathoms (more than 200 meters). Photo: G. Lewbel.

Tufts of brilliant sponges are common along the tops of the coral ramparts that line the drop off at Palancar. Photo: G. Lewbel.

one dive or twenty, since the reef is tremendous in size, and charter operators frequently visit different areas of Palancar to provide variety for their clients. If you take pot luck, you won't be disappointed.

Strong currents are common in the area, and most boats operate unanchored, dropping divers off upstream of the dive site and picking them up at the other end. Stay together with your group and with your guides or divemasters to facilitate pickup once on the surface, and, as with any other wall dive, be sure to monitor your depth and time carefully, since other divers in your group may not dive the same profile you choose due to the "bottomless" nature of the vertical walls.

Typical depth range	:	50 feet (15 meters) minimum to unlimited (wall)
Expertise required	:	intermediate (with qualified instructor or divemaster) or advanced
Typical current conditions:		moderate to strong
Access	:	boat only

Santa Rosa Reef shares a number of features with Palancar, Colombia, and the other coral buttress areas on the lip of the dropoff. It has tall columns of coral with vertical walls cut by channels which slope from the white sand bottom on their shoreward side down near-vertical, terraced canyons on their seaward side. As on the other buttress reefs, enormous plate

Santa Rosa Reef, like Palancar and Colombia, is a series of coral escarpments on the edge of a vertical wall. As at the other walls, the current here is typically strong. Divers should stay close to their group and carefully monitor their own time and depth as others may be diving a different profile along the deep dropoff. Photo: L. Martin.

The wall at Santa Rosa is riddled with caves, grottos and tunnels that are among the best on the island. The insides of these are often home to spectacular filter feeders—vase, tube and rope sponges, and giant sea fans. Photo: L. Martin.

corals, mammoth-sized sea fans, and spectacular sponges are common at Santa Rosa. The best diving is along the seaward faces of the buttresses, where divers can look down into blue depths and up along sheer cliff sides. Santa Rosa does differ from the other reefs in the diversity and quality of its caverns and grottos, though. If you want photographs or views of divers silhouetted in the mouths of caves or dropping through narrow slots between vertical walls, this is your reef. Tame, hand-fed groupers are common here, too. Lately, several small blacktip sharks have frequented Santa Rosa.

Santa Rosa Reef is known for strong currents, so drift diving is the norm. As we mentioned for Colombia and Palancar, be sure to monitor your own depth and time, since other divers may follow different dive profiles up and down the walls. Stay together with your dive guides or divemasters and with your group, as live boating is typical and you will all be picked up (hopefully in a group) down-current from your starting spot.

Typical depth range	:	60 feet (18 meters) minimum to unlimited (wall)
Expertise required	:	intermediate (with qualified instructor or divemaster) or advanced
Typical current conditions:		moderate to strong
Access	:	boat only

Colombia Reef is one of the great coral buttress areas located along the lip of the dropoff toward the southern end of the island. Huge pillars of coral loom over white sand on the shoreward side and slope downward on the seaward side to successive terraces below them. The tops of the pillars are mostly in the 60–70 foot (18–20 meter) range, while the narrow passageways and channels between them open onto the nearly vertical faces of the seaward side. You will find gigantic plate corals and huge sponges interspersed with anemones, gorgonian sea fans, and a wide variety of other attached organisms. Many fish live among the pillars and in the holes, caves, and crevices formed by the reef. Photographers will probably want to set up for wide-angle work, at least on a first dive, as the three-dimensional relief of Colombia Reef is second to none in the world.

Colombia Reef is a continuation of the towering coral buttresses that characterize the reefs on the south end of the island. The coral formations are interspersed with broad sand channels. Photo: G. Lewbel.

Large gorgonians line the wall near the lip of the dropoff at Colombia Reef.
Photo: G. Lewbel.

The typical boat dive on Colombia Reef will be a drift dive, since strong currents are common here. Some protection from water movement can be had on the back side of pillars and in channels, but divers can expect to cover quite a distance on one tank. As on all other wall dives, your selection of depth can range from the tops of the pillars to whatever your own judgment (and your guide) will permit. Your boat will probably operate unanchored, picking up your group at the end of the dive, so be sure to stay together with your dive guides or divemasters and the rest of your group. It's a long way to shore! Current direction on Colombia is quite variable, and large eddies and swirls are typical.

Typical depth range	:	100 feet (30 meters) to unlimited (wall)
Typical current conditions:		strong
Expertise required	:	advanced, with specialized training in deep diving techniques
Access	:	boat only

Maracaibo Reef is a deep reef at the southern tip of the island. If you want to dive Maracaibo, you'll probably have to get together with enough people to charter a boat and captain for the day (rather than ride on an "open" boat). In general, the captains on the slower boats will refuse to dive Maracaibo, since the run there and back takes a full day. The boat trip is not only longer than to the other major reefs, but also deeper. All members of your party should be advanced, very experienced divers trained in deep-diving techniques. Due to its location, Maracaibo is less protected from weather and the ride there is often wet and rough, so if you're prone to seasickness you might sit this one out.

Maracaibo is a buttress reef, with the inshore edges of most buttresses at depths of 100 feet (30 meters) or more. The offshore wall lip is at least 120 feet (36 meters) deep in some locations, so watch your depth gauge! The coral formations of Maracaibo resemble the other large dropoff wall reefs (e.g., Palancar, Santa Rosa, Colombia), with tunnels and caves

Clubbed anemones are common on the deeper reefs. The top of the wall at Maracaibo is at 100 feet (30 meters) in most places, requiring advanced training in deep diving techniques. Photo: G. Lewbel.

The short, pencil-like growth at the end of this yellow sting ray's tail is its barb. Other types of rays, including eagle rays and manta rays are also common at Maracaibo Reef, as are various types of sharks. Photo: G. Lewbel.

and vertical walls interspersed with broad sand channels. Very large buttresses are typical of Maracaibo. It's not worth the trouble to get to Maracaibo just to see coral, however. You can see spectacular coral and sponges at the other reefs more easily, less expensively, and with a shorter boat ride.

Shark Watching, Maybe!

Many of the divers that go to Maracaibo go to see sharks. Sharks are frequently spotted at Maracaibo, but (just like that noise in your car that disappears when you take it to the mechanic) you can't count on them. Blacktips (several close-ly related species) are most common, but it is possible to encounter hammerheads, shortfin makos, lemons, tigers, or bulls. Keep in mind, though, that you pay your money and you take your chances. Some years few sharks are seen, and other years sharks are seen on most dives. Big schools of eagle rays and mantas have also been seen at Maracaibo.

La Ceiba Dropoff 18

Typical depth range	:	70 feet (21 meters) to unlimited (wall)
Typical current conditions:		strong
Expertise required	:	advanced
Access	:	concrete steps at south base of La Ceiba Hotel pier

Most of the wall drift dives on Cozumel can be made safely only from a boat due to their distance from shore. The La Ceiba Dropoff (and the La Villa Blanca Dropoff, described next), however, often can be dived from the beach. This dive is rated as suitable for advanced divers only, since it's a fairly long swim from shore to the dropoff. You should only make this dive when the current is running in a south-to-north direction, as there are no convenient exits immediately to the south of La Ceiba. You ought to walk out to the end of the International Pier to see which way the current is running before you make your dive, and to get a good idea of the distance you will have to swim to and from shore to make this dive. The lip of the wall is a few hundred feet seaward of the tip of the International Pier.

The wall between the La Ceiba Beach Hotel and the La Villa Blanca has a lip at about 70–80 feet (21–25 meters), although it gets deeper in some places. The wall slopes downward rapidly at an angle of 45° or more.

Bar jacks are often seen along La Ceiba Dropoff, which is directly in front of the La Ceiba Hotel. This wall is not dived as frequently as the deep reefs on the south end of the island, so the fish are less accustomed to people. Photo: L. Martin.

The scenery along the wall at La Ceiba Dropoff is dominated by huge sponges, such as this eight-foot (three-meter) specimen. Photo: G. Lewbel.

Most of the lip is fairly smooth compared to the wall edges further south at Santa Rosa and Palancar, for example. Instead of the huge coral buttresses of the southern reefs, this area is dominated by the enormous sponges. Big schools of jacks and queen angelfishes are common here, and since the area is not dived as frequently as the southern reefs, the fish are not particularly used to divers. They aren't gun-shy, but won't pose for your camera while waiting for a handout. In fact, if you're planning to bring your camera on this dive, you'll want a wide-angle lens if possible, since the current doesn't favor sitting in one spot to take macro shots.

If you're planning to make this dive from the shore, you should also take a look at the preferred exit (the La Villa Blanca pier) so that you will recognize it from the water, and you should also select several alternative exits farther north. There are many places to leave the water safely along the shore, and if you are down-current (north) of the La Villa Blanca pier at the end of the dive, it should be simple to get out at the next pier or beach that you drift by. The important thing to remember is not to fight the current; swim 90° to it in order to get near shore, then just drift along parallel to the beach until you are carried to a safe exit spot.

The best spot to begin this dive from the shore is at the La Ceiba pier. There is a full-service dive shop at the La Ceiba Hotel. Swim straight out on the surface past the north end of the International Pier (be careful of vessels—read the dive entitled International Pier for additional cautions). The edge of the dropoff should be clearly visible from the surface as a color change from light to very dark blue. The swim from shore will probably take you about 15–20 minutes if you're in good shape. If you're diving from a boat, you should jump in directly offshore of the La Ceiba pier. Descend just inshore of the lip onto white sand at about 70 feet (21 meters) and ride the current toward the north, staying above or inshore of the dropoff lip. This dive is extremely exciting when the current is strong, and you may see half a mile or more of the lip of the dropoff on a single tank without doing any swimming except to and from the lip.

Boat Diving

Boat divers can stay on the lip as long as bottom time and air permit. A common, effective technique for maintaining a safe depth in this clear, clear water is to lower a line from your boat (or buoy, if you're shore diving) with a weight at your intended maximum dive depth. You then simply drift insight of the line, making sure you stay above the weight. If you're diving from a boat, ask the captain to stay parallel to and just inshore of the lip. If you're towing a buoy, you can pull the line to keep it along the lip with you.

If you're diving from shore, the best strategy is to leave the lip at about the half-way point in your dive profile, and swim straight toward shore. You will be carried northward on your inward swim, and will probably run low on air or bottom time while still up-current (south) of La Villa Blanca Hotel pier. If the current is very light (rarely is this the case), you could get out at your entry spot or at the Sol Caribe Hotel pier, but we've always been carried too far north to get back out at the Sol Caribe. Plan on taking a long ride with the current, and don't dawdle while inward bound or you'll miss your exit. An easy way to get to the sandy beach at La Villa Blanca is to swim through the shallow sand channels on both sides of the base of the pier. Stay clear of coral heads and over sand to avoid urchins. The channels are narrow, so be careful. If you end up north of the Villa Blanca, there are several alternative exits at the La Perla Hotel pier and (much farther north) the Galapago Inn pier. There are full-service dive shops at both the La Villa Blanca and the Galapago Inn in case you need a refill for the next dive.

Sponges grow under a ledge on the downcurrent side of a coral head. Photo: L. Martin.

75

Typical depth range	:	70 feet (21 meters) to unlimited (wall)
Typical current conditions:		strong
Expertise required	:	advanced
Access	:	beach in front of the La Villa Blanca Hotel, or via boat

As we mentioned when describing the La Ceiba Dropoff, the majority of the wall drift dives on Cozumel are too far from shore to be dived except from a boat. The La Villa Blanca Dropoff often can be dived from the beach, though, and it's slightly closer to shore than the La Ceiba dropoff. Nonetheless, this dive is rated as suitable for advanced divers only, since it's still a long swim from shore to the dropoff. You should only make this dive when the current is running in a south-to-north direction. If the current is from the north, you may be carried southward of La Ceiba, and there are no convenient exits immediately to the south of La Ceiba. You ought to walk out to the end of the International Pier to see which way the

Among the many denizens of La Villa Blanca Dropoff   are large and subtly colored gray angelfish. Photo: G. Lewbel.

As at La Ceiba Dropoff, the bottom at La Villa Blanca Dropoff ends in a steep slope, rather than a sheer cliff as at the southern reefs. Big sponges and pelagic fish are the primary attractions for divers drifting with the strong current at La Villa Blanca.
Photo: G. Lewbel.

current is running before you make your dive, and to get a good idea of the distance you will have to swim to and from shore to make this dive. The lip of the La Villa Blanca Dropoff is about as far offshore as the tip of the International Pier.

The wall between the La Villa Blanca and the Galapago Inn is a continuation of the wall described for the La Ceiba Dropoff, but tends to be a bit deeper. The lip is mostly at about 80 feet (25 meters), though some areas are deeper. The dropoff is a slope of about 45° or more rather than a sheer precipice. Occasional patches of coral are mixed with groups of very large sponges, and schools of big pelagic fishes often cruise along the lip. If you're bringing photo gear, you'll probably want to use a setup that does not require much focusing (e.g., wide angle), since you'll be ripping along in the current too fast to do much fiddling with your camera.

If you're planning to make this dive from the shore, you should also take a look at the preferred exit (the Galapago Inn pier) so that you will recognize it from the water, and you should also select several alternative exits farther north. If you are down-current (north) of the Galapago Inn pier at the end of the dive, it should be simple to get out at the next pier or beach that you drift by. Don't fight the current; swim 90° to it in order to get near shore, then just drift along parallel to the beach until you are carried to a safe exit spot.

The best spot to begin this dive from shore is the small pier at the La Villa Blanca Hotel. There is a full-service dive shop at the base of the pier. Swim out through the shallow sand channels at either side of the pier, watching out for urchins. Swim straight offshore on the surface (be careful of vessels). The edge of the dropoff should be clearly visible from the surface as a color change from light to very dark blue. It's about a 15–20 minute swim to the dropoff. If you're diving from a boat, you should jump in directly offshore of the La Villa Blanca pier. Descend just inshore of the lip onto white sand at about 80 feet (25 meters), and drift with the current toward the north, staying above or just inshore of the lip. If the current is strong, you'll then cover a great deal of distance without much effort. The weighted line described for the La Ceiba Dropoff will be helpful in maintaining safe depths on this dive.

Boat divers can stay on the lip as long as bottom time and air permit. If you're diving from shore, you should plan to leave the lip at about the half-way point in your dive profile, and swim steadily straight toward shore. You will be carried northward on your inward swim, and will

A diver discovers a heart urchin in the sand flats en route to the dropoff. Photo: L. Martin.

A tangled mass of multi-colored sponges decorates a coral head. Photo: G. Lewbel.

probably run low on air or bottom time while still up-current (south) of the Galapago Inn pier. If the current is very light (rarely is this the case), you could get out at your entry spot or at the La Perla Hotel pier, but we've always been carried too far north to get back out at the La Perla. The Galapago Inn has a concrete channel entryway and steps on its northern pier. Swim just to the right of the pier and into the protected channel, and then walk out. Be careful of urchins on adjacent rocks. If you end up north of the Galapago Inn, there are several alternative exits at the Barracuda Hotel pier and the many beaches in town near the central plaza. There is a full-service dive shop that can refill your tank at the Galapago Inn, and many shops in town.

3

Marine Life

Cozumel has the usual suite of Caribbean reef fish, invertebrates, and plants. Although space does not permit a detailed listing of species, a few of the animals likely to be seen are described in this section. Divers will notice a definite zonation of groups of species that change with increasing depth and distance from shore. The zonation reflects decreasing levels of light and wave exposure with increasing depth, and increasing current velocities offshore. The zonation is most obvious among such reef-forming invertebrates as corals and sponges, but many fish are closely associated with the reef-builders and so show zonation themselves.

Corals. Very close to shore, perhaps the most prominent species is the elkhorn coral. It forms huge colonies that shelter long-spined sea urchins during the daytime. At night, the urchins move away from their shelters and graze on plants on the surrounding bottom. The largest gorgonians, or sea fans and sea whips, are near shore too. Divers are more likely to encounter fire coral in shallow water, growing on gorgonian skeletons, dead coral, or other surfaces.

Farther from shore, most of the reefs are dominated by the mountainous star coral and the cavernous star coral.

In shallow water, these tend to grow as large mounds. As you probably know, corals are animals, but they have internal plants *(zooxanthellae)* which produce food and oxygen that are used by their hosts. The zooxanthellae need light to exist, and many species of corals change their growth forms depending on where they live in order to capture as much light as possible for their zooxanthellae. As a result, in deeper water (where there is not as much light) species such as the star corals tend to form sheets or plates that act like natural solar collectors. The large buttresses, such as those on Palancar Reef, are built mainly by star corals,

A feathery basket star opens up at night at La Ceiba Reef Preserve and Trail. Many underwater creatures are only visible, or best seen, at night. Photo: L. Martin. ▶

and the various growth forms can be seen at different depths. Species can always be recognized by the shape of the individual polyps, whatever the shape of the entire colony. The massive corals, such as the giant brain coral, are found over a wide depth range but are often larger in deeper water.

Other corals, such as the sheet or plate corals, specialize in living in low-light situations (crevices, overhangs or deep water). These corals can become very large, thin, and fragile at depths where they are not likely to be broken by waves.

Anemones and Sponges. The common clubbed anemone frequently is seen with fluorescent tentacle tips. These tentacles bear the stinging cells with which this animal captures tiny crustaceans and other prey. Different colored tentacles do not indicate different species but rather color phases of the same species.

There are sponges wherever coral is found in Cozumel, and large sponges can be seen on nearly every dive. Look for the brittle stars in the purple vase sponges. Bristle worms (also called fire worms) are common everywhere, but can be seen breeding on purple vase sponges at night during the late fall. The most spectacular sponges that divers can see around Cozumel are the flat red sheets that grow on the vertical walls of the International Pier and the barrel sponges on the dropoffs. The red sheet sponges look brown by daylight but are blood-red by night or in strobe-lit photographs. The barrel sponges on the dropoffs have grown into funnel shapes under the influence of the usual south-to-north current. Their open cavities face north so that more stagnant water (carrying wastes from the sponge) is extracted from the funnel by the passing current, and water with food and oxygen surrounds the outer filtering surface of the sponge.

Fishes. Fishes on Cozumel are extremely diverse, and most of the abundant reef species in the Caribbean can be seen at one time or another by divers on Cozumel. A few common nearshore species include yellow stingrays, barracudas, black groupers (handfed and tamed by divers on Palancar and Santa Rosa reefs), moray eels, angelfishes, butterfly fishes, wrasses, barjacks, grunts, snappers, and triggerfish. Chubs and yellow and black barred sergeant-majors will surround you, begging for food. Damselfishes will nip at you on every reef, and various parrotfishes can be seen and heard breaking coral with their jaws. Bigeye, glasseye snappers, and glassy sweepers are often seen hiding in shaded crevices in the daytime. Most photographers will want to search under coral heads at the edge of sandy patches for the elusive splendid, toadfish, a magnificent species in a family of fishes otherwise not known for their beauty. The splendid toadfish is believed to be common only in the vicinity of Cozumel Island. While looking under ledges for toadfish, you may find large spiny lobsters and crabs but note the following section if you're tempted to take dinner.

Spearfishing and Hunting Underwater

Most of the island's diveable reefs lie within a Mexican national preserve. This preserve extends from the area of the La Ceiba Hotel southward to the tip of the island, including Palancar, Colombia, Santa Rosa, and other well-known reefs. Collection of any animals (including shells with living inhabitants) or plants within the preserve is strictly forbidden. North of the La Ceiba, sport fishing is allowed if you have a Mexican fishing license.

The Mexican game fishing regulations are fairly complex, and include bag and seasonal restrictions on many species. Scuba could be used for collecting fish and lobsters as of this printing. Fishing licenses can be requested from the Oficina de Pesca (Fish Office) in San Miguel on Cozumel Island (ask a taxi driver where it is) but are best obtained in advance from the Oficina de Pesca, 1010 Second Avenue, Suite 1605, San Diego, CA 92101, telephone (619) 233-6956. Prices for the licenses currently are changing but have been nominal in the past for short trips. Take the time to ask for a copy of the most recent regulations, though, and ask specifically about diving requirements. Even if you have a license with you, go to the Oficina de Pesca in San Miguel and inquire about local regulations. Be careful! The Mexican government takes illegal collecting very seriously, and a large fine including the gear used for the collection (i.e., all of your diving equipment and the boat!) would not be out of the ordinary.

Gray snappers congregate under a ledge at Chanakab. If you plan to do spearfishing, be sure you are not in a preserve (Chanakab is protected) and have a valid license. Photo: G.S. Boland.

4

Safety

This section discusses common hazards, including dangerous marine animals, and emergency procedures in case of a diving accident. We do not discuss the diagnosis or treatment of serious medical problems; refer to your first aid manual or emergency diving accident manual for that information.

We also suggest some ways to contact qualified medical personnel as rapidly as possible, based partly on responses to our own inquiries for this volume and partly on information supplied by other sources. The telephone numbers and addresses given in this edition were current to the best of the authors' knowledge in the late 1983, but the authors assume no responsibility for assuring that phone numbers or contact information are correct. Emergency contact information can change unpredictably when personnel and facilities move, get new telephone numbers, and so on. Readers are advised to check on emergency contact information during or just before the time of their dive trip.

It is very important to be well versed at using decompression tables, especially on Cozumel where most diving tends to be deep. Here divers are decompressing before returning to their boat. Photo: G. Lewbel.

A well-camouflaged spotted scorpionfish rests almost motionless on a rocky surface. These creatures have poisonous spines which can inflict extremely painful and often dangerous wounds. Watch where you place your hands and feet; these are difficult fishes to spot. If you are stung, see a doctor at once. Photo: G. Lewbel. ▶

Diving Accidents

In case of a diving accident such as a lung overpressure injury (e.g., air embolism, pneumothorax, mediastinal emphysema) or decompression sickness ("bends"), prompt recompression treatment in a chamber may be essential to prevent permanent injury or death.

Local Facilities. There is a recompression chamber within a few blocks of the water at the Hospital *(Centro de Salud)*, phone number 2-01-40. Pick up a local map when you arrive to pinpoint its location, or ask one of the residents to point it out to you. The Hospital is one of the largest buildings in town, just east of the municipal power plant on a road that intersects the shoreline road near the Barracuda Hotel.

The dive operators on the island are familiar with the chamber and know how to contact it via radio *"La Costera* (Coast Guard), Channel 16" as well as by telephone. In light of the necessity for clear communication without language barriers, it may be fastest to ask the nearest dive operator or dive shop to make the necessary arrangements. Any particular operator you dive with should take responsibility for assisting you in every way possible.

You will have to decide whether to accept treatment at this chamber by local personnel, or whether you prefer to risk a flight to an alternative chamber such as one of those along the United States coast of the Gulf of Mexico. Previous reports from the Cozumel chamber have been mixed. Apparently, oxygen and full-scale treatments have not always been available to divers at the Cozumel chamber. In addition, should a chamber treatment not result in complete recovery, you will either have to undergo local hospital care or risk an aircraft flight back home while still suffering bends symptoms. In recent months we have been told that major improvements were scheduled for the facilities, but we have not personally confirmed the present status of the chamber. A brief visit to the Hospital and a tour of the chamber would be time well spent, both to learn the location and current condition of the chamber and to check on the state of readiness of its personnel.

U.S. Facilities. Whether or not you choose to accept local treatment, our recommendation is that you contact the Divers Alert Network (DAN) in the United States immediately in case of a diving injury.

DAN. The Divers Alert Network (DAN), a membership association of individuals and organizations sharing a common interest in diving safety operates a **24-hour national hotline, (919) 684-8111** (collect calls are accepted in an emergency). DAN does not directly provide medical care, however, they do provide advice on early treatment, evacuation, and hyperbaric treatment of diving related injuries. Additionally, DAN provides diving safety information to members to help prevent accidents. Membership is $10 a year, offering: the DAN *Underwater Diving Accident Manual,* describing symptoms and first aid for the major diving related injuries and emergency room guidelines for drugs and i.v. fluids; a membership card listing diving related symptoms on one side and DAN's emergency and non emergency phone numbers on the other; 1 tank decal and 3 small equipment decals with DAN's logo and emergency number; and a newsletter, "Alert Diver", describes diving medicine and safety information in layman's language with articles for professionals, case histories, and medical questions related to diving. Special memberships for dive stores, dive clubs, and corporations are also available. The DAN manual can be purchased for $4 from the Administrative Coordinator, National Diving Alert Network, Duke University Medical Center, Box 3823, Durham, NC 27710.

DAN divides the U.S. into 7 regions, each coordinated by a specialist in diving medicine who has access to the skilled hyperbaric chambers in his region. Non emergency or information calls are connected to the DAN office and information number, (919) 684-2948. This number can be dialed direct, Monday-Friday between 9 a.m. and 5 p.m. Eastern Standard time. Divers should not call DAN for general information on chamber locations.

Chamber status changes frequently making this kind of information dangerous if obsolete at the time of an emergency. Instead, divers should contact DAN as soon as a diving emergency is suspected. All divers should have comprehensive medical insurance and check to make sure that hyperbaric treatment and air ambulance services are covered internationally.

Diving is a safe sport and there are very few accidents compared to the number of divers and number of dives made each year. But when the infrequent injury does occur, DAN is ready to help. DAN, originally 100% federally funded, is now largely supported by the diving public. Membership in DAN or purchase of DAN manuals or decals provides divers with useful safety information and provides DAN with necessary operating funds. Donations to DAN are tax deductible as DAN is a legal non-profit public service organization.

Air Ambulance Service. If you elect to leave Cozumel for treatment, you are probably going to need a chartered flight with medical equipment and personnel on board, in an aircraft capable of pressurization at the equivalent of sea-level (1 atmosphere). A number of air ambulance companies in the United States can provide this service, but flying in Mexico requires some red tape that is best taken care of in advance. Under ideal circumstances you will probably wait at least three hours after you request an aircraft before it lands in Cozumel.

Two well-known air ambulance operators have made arrangements for a speedy transit in and out of Mexican airspace. They are 1) Life Flight, headquartered in Houston, Texas: 24-hour emergency phone numbers (800) 392-4357 and (713) 797-4357; and 2) Air-Evac International, headquartered near San Diego, California: 24-hour emergency phone numbers (619) 278-3822 and (800) 854-2569.

You should be aware that the cost of an evacuation flight will be high and that payment will be expected either in Mexico or promptly after arrival in the States. You will most likely be asked to provide proof of financial responsibility in the form of cash, check, or credit cards, or·to furnish names and phone numbers of friends or relatives in the States who will guarantee the cost of the flight. Brace yourself for a bill that may run $5,000 (US) or more, depending on how fast an aircraft you need (this may be your chance to ride in a Lear Jet), what medical equipment and personnel need to be on board, its point of origin, and its destination.

Emergency Contacts

Recompression Chamber (Cozumel)	: Tel. 2-01-40 Radio: La Costera (Coast Guard), Channel 16 (canál numero diez y seis)
Divers' Alert Network (DAN) (for assistance in dealing with Cozumel recompression chamber or for finding a chamber in U.S.)	: (919) 684-8111
Air ambulance services (to U.S. recompression chambers) Life Flight (Houston, TX)	: (800) 392-4357; (713) 797-4357
Air-Evac International (S. Diego, CA)	: (800) 854-2567; (619) 278-3822

Common Hazardous Marine Animals

Sea Urchins. The most common hazardous animal divers will encounter around Cozumel is the long-spined sea urchin. This urchin has spines that are capable of penetrating wetsuits, booties, and gloves like a knife through butter. Injuries are nearly always immediately painful, and sometimes infect. Urchins are found at every diving depth, although they are more common in shallow water near shore, especially under coral heads. At night the urchins come out of their hiding places and are even easier to bump into. Minor injuries can be dealt with by extracting the spines (easier said than done!) and treating the wound with antibiotic cream. Make sure your tetanus immunization is current; serious punctures will require a doctor's attention. The easiest way to find a doctor is to go to the Hospital (see the first section of this chapter), or to ask any hotel desk to call one for you.

Fire Coral. Fire coral is most common in shallow water, but can grow as an encrusting form on dead gorgonians or coral at any depth. Contact with fire coral causes a burning feeling which usually goes away in a minute or two. In some individuals, contact results in red welts. Cortisone cream can reduce the inflammation. Coral cuts and scrapes also can irritate and frequently infect. We've treated minor coral scratches successfully with antibiotic cream, but serious cuts should be handled by a doctor, especially if broken bits of coral are embedded in the wound.

Bristle or Fire Worms. Bristle worms, also called fire worms, can be found on most reefs with a little searching. If you touch one with bare skin it will embed tiny, stinging bristles in your skin and cause a burning sensation that may be followed by the development of a red spot or welt. The sensation is similar to touching fire coral or massaging one of those fuzzy, soft-looking cactuses on land. The bristles will eventually work their way out of your skin in a couple of days. You can try to scrape them off with the edge of a sharp knife. Cortisone cream helps reduce local inflammation.

Sponges. Sponges also have fine spicules, and some species (so-called fire sponges) have a chemical irritant that is immediately painful. Although bright red color is sometimes a clue to the bad ones, it's not completely reliable. We have been stung by various innocuous-looking sponges. If you get spicules in your skin, try scraping them off with the edge of a sharp knife. We've also tried pouring mild vinegar solutions and mild ammonia solutions on the parts that hurt; sometimes they work, sometimes they don't. The stinging sensation usually goes away within a day, and cortisone cream helps.

Rays. Sand flats around Cozumel are inhabited by two species of sting rays, the southern sting ray (very large, wary, and difficult to approach), and the yellow sting ray, (small, well-camouflaged, and easy to approach). Sting rays are not especially aggressive, but they don't take kindly to being sat on, patted, or stepped on. If you leave them alone, they'll leave you alone. If you insist on a 1:1 macro shot of a sting ray nostril you will probably be stung by the long, barbed stinger at the base of the tail. Wounds are always extremely painful, are often deep and infective, and can cause serious symptoms including anaphylactic shock. If you get stung, head for the Hospital and ask a doctor to take care of the wound.

Moray Eels. Moray eels are dangerous only if harassed. There are lots of morays under coral heads and in crevices. In recent years, divers at other islands have hand-fed morays, but this practice has not yet become widespread on Cozumel. One of the authors who was involved in a scientific fish-tagging experiment can attest personally to the biting ability of green morays (number of needle-like teeth, penetration depth, number of stitches required, etc.). If you watch where you stick your hands, however, you will not have to test Mexican morays' dispositions. Bites are sometimes infective and very painful and call for a doctor's attention.

Stonefishes. Stonefishes or scorpionfishes are well-camouflaged, small fish (usually less than a foot long) that have poisonous spines hidden among their fins. They are often difficult to spot, since they typically sit quietly on the bottom looking more like plant-covered rocks than fish. As with sting rays, watch where you put your hands and knees and you're not likely to meet one the hard way. If you get stung, severe allergic reactions are quite possible and great pain and infection are virtually certain, so head for the Hospital and see a doctor.

Sharks. We are not aware of any reported shark attacks at Cozumel. Sharks are very uncommon at most of the reefs around Cozumel but several small blacktips recently have taken up residence near Santa Rosa Reef. Sharks are also seen more often at Maracaibo Reef than other sites, and nurse sharks are sometimes spotted sleeping under ledges at Yocab and San Juan Reefs. Please don't tug on nurse sharks' tails while they are asleep, by the way, even though it's tempting. They wake up grumpy and have bitten a number of divers in other locations. Any shark injury obviously calls for immediate medical attention.

Barracuda. Barracudas are included in this section only because of their undeserved reputation for ferocity. There are a few unconfirmed reports of attacks on swimmers in dirty water in other locations, but you'll have nothing to worry about on Cozumel. You'll be lucky to get one close enough for a good photograph. They're rather timid about coming closer than a few yards. At night, though, you can sometimes get within touching distance of a sleeping barracuda. If you want to see schools of smaller barracudas, try a dive near the International Pier. If you want to see very large barracudas, try Barracuda Reef (naturally!).

Appendix 1: List of Services

As we mentioned in Chapter 1, "Overview of Cozumel," there are a few problems that seem to crop up again and again for divers on Cozumel. Most of these problems are related to lodging. Making reservations in Mexico has always been a bit tricky, but it is more so than ever at this time. Since the peso has been declining in value with respect to the U.S. dollar, the occasional holiday rush has been replaced with a steady onslaught of American divers wanting to take advantage of low Mexican prices and a favorable exchange rate. At the same time, hotels and diving facilities that purchase supplies and equipment from the States have been caught in a bind; their pesos buy fewer dollars, and Mexico has been suffering from an inflation rate averaging well over 50% a year for most goods.

As a result of all the confusion, it is extremely important for the hotels to have every room occupied if at all possible since they are making less money per person. A number of Cozumel's hotels have responded to this pressure by "overbooking," that is, selling more rooms than they have available.

At this time, therefore, we must recommend against counting on individual reservations with hotels on Cozumel unless you have paid for the rooms in advance, have written receipts with you from the hotel showing dates of arrival and departure and amount paid, and are sufficiently familiar with the hotel that you know they will honor your reservation. We also recommend that all correspondence by mail with Mexico be sent Registered, especially if bearing checks or other items of value.

Hotels

Hotels with which we are personally familiar and which have been, on the whole, satisfactory to us as travelers and as divers have been marked with an asterisk (*). The asterisk thus represents the authors' preferences only. As we have not stayed in every hotel, the lack of an asterisk does not necessarily indicate that the facility or service is unsatisfactory.

All of the hotels on the island can be contacted by mail using the hotel's name followed by "Cozumel, Q. Roo, Mexico. The local phone number is given in the table. As we indicated above, it's a small town. The letter S indicates a location (see Chapter 1, Overview of Cozumel) to the south of town, that is, nearest the main reef systems (Palancar, Colombia, Santa Rosa). This is the most desirable area since the boat ride is shortest to the reefs. The letter C indicates a condominium or apartment-rental-style facility. The letter D indicates full-service dive shop on premises. The letter L indicates luxury-class facility.

HOTEL ACCOMMODATIONS

Name	Phone Number	Special Notes
*Aguilar	——	simple, clean, economical
Bahia	2-02-09	
Barracuda	2-00-02	D
Cabanas del Caribe	2-00-72	
*Condumel	2-08-92	C, luxurious condos
*Divers' Inn	2-01-45	S, C, D,
El Marques	2-05-37	
El Presidente	2-03-89	near Paraiso Reef, nice beach S, L, D,
Fiesta Cozumel	2-05-22	
*Galapago Inn	2-06-63	S, D, simple, clean
La Perla	2-01-88	
La Villa Blanca	2-07-30	S, D
*La Ceiba	2-03-79	S, L, D, underwater airplane and ecology trail, near Paraiso Reef, Intenational Pier
Maya Cozumel	2-00-11	
Mayan Plaza	2-04-11	
Sol Caribe	2-07-00	S, L, D, near airplane and ecology trail, nice beach
Suites Colonial	2-05-06	
*Vista Del Mar	2-05-45	simple, clean, economical

Key:
* Indicates authors' preference
C Indicates condominiums/apartment-rental facilities
D Indicates full service dive shop on premises

L Indicates luxury class
S Indicates shortest distance to reefs

Dive Shops and Dive Operators

For dive shops and operators, we have listed only those with which we are personally familiar and with which we have been previously satisfied.

DIVE SHOPS

Shop/Operator	Phone Number	Special Notes
*Aqua Safari	2-01-01, 2-06-61	In town, B, T, I
*Blue Angel	2-07-30	At La Villa Blanca Hotel, I
*Dive Cozumel	2-07-30, 2-10-46	At La Villa Blanca Hotel, B, T
*Dive Cozumel		At Divers' Inn, B, T, I
*Galapago Inn	2-06-63	At Galapago Inn, B, T, I
*Fantasia Divers	2-07-80	At La Ceiba and Sol Caribe Hotels, B, T, I
*Scuba Cozumel	2-06-27, 2-08-53	In town, B, T, I

Key:
B Indicates boat diving
T Indicates tank rental

I Indicates instructions available

Appendix 2: Further Reading

The most accessible information on Cozumel Island (other than this guide) can be found in articles in *Ocean Realm* and *Skin Diver* magazines. Both magazines cover Cozumel every year or two. If you don't subscribe to one of these publications you can probably find at least one of them in your local library, and most dive shops that run trips to Cozumel maintain a file of clippings. However, magazine articles and books go out of date, needless to say. It's hard to find published articles that are current on hotels, dive operators, and other topside facilities. On Cozumel, personnel and facilities change very rapidly compared to other Caribbean Islands. By the time material is published, it may already contain inaccuracies even though it was correct at the time it was written.

The most consistently reliable sources about Cozumel's hotels, dive operators, and other topside facilities are dive travel specialists and dive shop owners who have been there recently. The dive travel industry must keep up with the local scene, since reservations and bookings have to be correct. A call or visit to someone who just spent a week on the island will provide you with more useful information than via almost any other means.

To learn more about the fish and corals you will see while diving around Cozumel, we recommend that you purchase a copy of Idaz and Jerry Greenberg's book, *Guide to Corals and Fishes of Florida, the Bahamas, and the Caribbean,* published by Seahawk Press, 6840 SW 92nd Street, Miami, Florida 33156. The book, available from most diveshops in the States as well as on the island, is available in a waterproof version you can take underwater, as well as a topside version. For more detail, we suggest Patrick Colin's Book, "Caribbean Reef Invertebrates and Plants", from TFH Publications, Inc., P.O. Box 27, Neptune City, New Jersey 07753.

Index

Accidents, 86-88
Air ambulance services, 88
Algae, 58, **59**
Anemones, 35, 41, **43**, 68, **70**, 82
Angelfish, 35, 47, 73, **76**

Bar jacks, 72, 73
Barracuda, 41, 90
Barracuda Reef, 60-61
Beachcomber Cavern, 52-55
Bermuda chub, 37
Bigeyes, 35, 54
Blue chromis fishes, 45
Boat diving, 74
Brain coral, **54**
Bristle worms, 82, 89
Brittle stars, 82
Buoyancy control, 26-27

Cardinalfish, **58**, 59
Cardona Reef, 58-59
C-card, 21
Chankanab, 50-51
Colombia Reef, 68-69
Colombia Shallows, 62-63
Conch, 35, 48
Coral butresses, 63, 64, 66, **66**, 68, **68**, 70-71
Coral heads, 45, **46**, 47, **47**, 51, 56, 57, **57**, 58, 74, **79**
Corals, **22**, 80, 80-82, 82. See also specific type
Crabs, **34**, 57
Currency, 18
Currents, 24, 27, 45, 48, 57, 61, 65, 69, 73-74, 77-78

Damselfish, 37
DAN (Divers Alert Network), 86-87, 88
Decompression sickness, 86-88
Deep diving, 70
Dining, 19
Dive boats, **27**, 28-29, **29**
Dive operators, 28-29, 92
Dive shops, 36, 37, 50, 78, 79, 92
Diving techniques, 24-27
Drift diving, 24, 27, 47, 57, 67,69
Driver's license, 20
Drums, 51, **51**

Elkhorn coral, **32**, 33, 37
Emergency contacts, 88

Filefish, 35, 47
Finger coral, 61

Fire coral, 41, 89
Fire worms, 82, 89
Fishes, 82. See also specific type
Fishing licenses, 83
Fungus, 54

Glasseye snappers, 54, 59
Glassy sweepers, 54, 59
Gorgonian Flats, 32-33, 39
Gorgonians, 37, **38**
Green Mirror, 55
Groupers, 54, 67
Grunts, **49**, 51

Hazards. See Safety
Horse-eye jacks, 61
Horseshoe, the (la Herradura), 64
Hotels, 15, 16-17, 91-92
Hunting underwater, 83

International Pier, **16**, **22**, 40-43, **43**
Ironshore, 14, 24

Jacknife fishes, 51

Kits Mound, 51

La Ceiba Dropoff, 72-75
La Ceiba Hotel, **15**
La Ceiba Hotel pier, **26**
La Ceiba Reef Preserve and Trail, 36-37, **81**
La Villa Blanca Dropoff, 76-79
Leaf coral, **32**
Lettuce coral, 37
Licenses, 20, 83
Live boat techniques, 24
Lobsters, 35, 57
Lung overpressure injury, 86-88

Madonna, sculptured bronze, 51
Maracaibo Reef, 70-71
Marine life, 80-83
    hazardous, 89-90
Mayan culture, 12
Moray eels, **40**, 41, 90

Natural history, 14-15
Night diving, 37, 46, 50
Nocturnal fishes, 35, 41, 54, 59

Oysters, 48

Palancar Gardens, 64
Palancar Reef, 64-65
Paraiso Reef North, 44-45

Paraiso Reef South, 42, 46-49
Parrotfish, 33, 38, 58
Patch reefs, 60
Pelagic fishes, 77, **77**
Pen shells, 48
Pier diving, 36-37
Pillar coral, 37
Pino's Bowl, 61
Plate coral, 37, 66-67
Pufferfish, 41

Rating systems, 10, 19, 31
Rays, 35, 40, **71**, 90
Recompression treatment, 86-88

Safety, 42, 53, 84-90
San Francisco Reef, 34-35
San Juan Reef, 60-61
San Miguel, 15, **18**
Santa Rosa Reef, 66-67
Scorpion fish, 84, 85
Sea biscuits, **40**, 41
Sea cucumbers, 41, **46**, 47
Sea fans, 32, 33, 67, 68, **69**
Sea turtle shells, **21**
Sea urchins, **32**, 33, 54, **58**, 74, 79, 89
Sergeant-majors, 38
Sharks, 61, 67, 71, 90
Shopping, 20, 29, 92
Shore diving, 24, 29
Silver fingerlings, **52**
Snappers, 51, 54, 59, **83**
Spearfishing, 83
Sponges, **22**, **36**, 37, 41, **43**, 45, **45**, **47**, 61, 63, **65**, 67, 71, 73, **73**, 75, 77, **77**, **79**, 82, 89
Squirrelfish, 47, 59
Star coral, 37, **80**
Starfish, **22**, **41**
Stonefishes, 90
Sunken Airplane, 28-29, 37
Sweepers, 35, 54, 59

Taxis, 17, 24
Tilefish, 37, 63
Tipping, 17
Toadfish, **44**, 45
Tortoise shells, **21**
Tourist Permit, 20
Transportation, 17, 24
Travel documents, 21
Trumpet fish, 35
Trunkfishes, **56**

Wall dive techniques, 26-27
Weather, 14

Yocab Reef, 56-57

94

FREE   FREE   FREE

Now that you have worked all the problems in this book, you will want to protect it for future reference.

Send for your FREE WATERPROOF ENCLOSURE by completing the coupon below and sending it to:

Pisces Books
P.O. Box 678
Locust Valley, NY 11560

Pisces Books
P.O. Box 678
Locust Valley, NY 11560

Please send me my free waterproof enclosure.

I have been diving for _____ years.

I make about _____ out-of-state dive trips per year.

Name _____

Address _____

City _____ State _____ Zip _____